мыновление на шаицау.

Dawn MacLeod Wilson
July 1991

The
Peter Owen
Anthology

A drawing from *Stories and Drawings*, Roland Topor

The Peter Owen Anthology

FORTY YEARS OF INDEPENDENT PUBLISHING

Selected and with an Introduction by
Peter Owen

FOREWORD BY D. J. ENRIGHT

PETER OWEN
London and Chester Springs PA

PETER OWEN PUBLISHERS
73 Kenway Road London SW5 0RE

Peter Owen Books are distributed in the USA by
Dufour Editions Inc. Chester Springs PA 19425-0449

The contents of this volume © Peter Owen 1991

British Library Cataloguing in Publication Data
The Peter Owen anthology: forty years of independent
publishing.
1. Literature – Anthologies
I. Owen, Peter
808.8
ISBN 0-7206-0810-4

Typesetting by Rowland Phototypesetting of
Bury St Edmunds Suffolk
Printed in Great Britain by Billings of Worcester

Contents

Illustrations

ILLUSTRATIONS

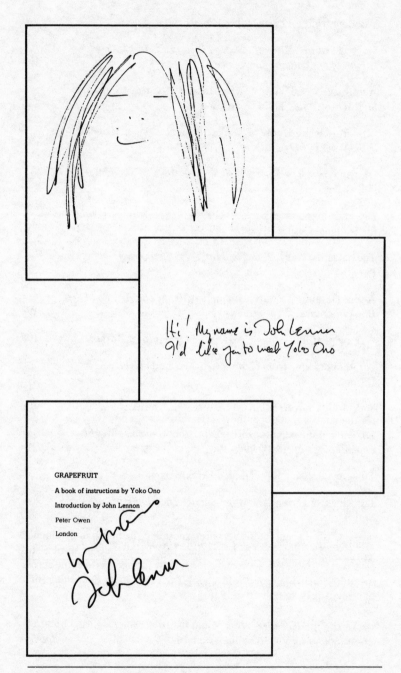

Title page, inscription and original drawing in Peter Owen's own copy of
Grapefruit, Yoko Ono

Foreword

D. J. ENRIGHT

THE YEAR 1951 MUST HAVE BEEN A RELATIVELY GOOD TIME TO START A publishing venture. In those far-off days publishing (including promotion) was more 'amateur' (a dirty word which may soon become clean again) and less 'competitive', and you could sell books without the aid of a huge and cripplingly expensive marketing operation. By way of justifying the latter, today's big publishers tell us that publishing is a global business. Where the finding of authors is concerned, it was always global for Peter Owen, though perhaps not always what would unequivocally be termed business.

No doubt he has had his difficulties. My experiences as an author and – mercifully more brief – as a publisher suggest that by and large there is little to choose between authors and publishers. Friedrich Hebbel, the nineteenth-century German writer, said: 'It is easier to walk on the waters with Christ than to get along with a publisher'; publishers have felt the same way about authors. If Barabbas was a publisher, then Judas could have been an author. Equally, Christ might have been an author, gifted but risky, and John the Baptist a perceptive and attentive publisher, who met an unfortunate end.

While in this biblical strain, we might note that the *Frankfurter Allgemeine Zeitung* once described Peter Owen as a David among the conglomerate Goliaths which the economic disease of gigantism has thrown up. Not all those Goliaths are Philistines; whatever the potency of the balance sheet, publishers are exposed to the improving influence of their better authors. The figures may tend to kill, but the spirit is still alive and gives life. Or so we may hope. How strange it is to come across the following in Stanley Unwin's book *The Truth about Publishing* (first published in 1926, revised in 1946):

> . . . the tide has now turned, and many of the more discriminating authors have come to realize that better service can be obtained from publishers who can give personal attention to their work than from

firms where it will of necessity be merely one of a long list. The day of gauging a publisher's merits by the extent to which he will gamble on 'advance payments' in anticipation of royalties is passing. As Charles Morgan rightly says, 'a publisher's steady confidence is worth all the advances in the world.'

Emerson remarked that we are all 'discontented pendulums', and it is in the nature of pendulums to swing.

Small is not inevitably beautiful, and can be short-lived, but in literature, where pluralism – diversity of taste and judgement – is of the essence, a dozen small or moderate-sized publishers make for greater health than one large publisher. One man's poison is another's cup of tea. Stanley Unwin observed, 'If a publisher declines your manuscript, remember it is merely the decision of one fallible human being, and try another'; committees are equally, or more, fallible. I remember how a manuscript would arrive at the offices of Chatto & Windus/The Hogarth Press, addressed to Chatto, with an accompanying letter to the effect that the author so admired the Chatto list that he/she was offering his/her book to them and to no one else. By the same post a second copy of the manuscript, addressed to The Hogarth Press, would arrive with a letter to the effect that such was the author's admiration for The Hogarth Press that. . . . The fact that the two imprints shared the same premises failed to arouse suspicions in these authors – but after all they had the right idea. To find a buyer, shop around!

Ten years ago the distinguished American publisher Robert Giroux remarked that whereas publishers' editors used to be known by their authors, 'now some of them are known by their restaurants.' The situation has worsened since then, for nowadays you can't remember who it is they are currently working for. Peter Owen has been with the one firm for forty years! To have stayed in the same employment for five years is seen as a public disgrace these days: you must be such a fuddy-duddy that no one else will give you a job.

One danger in a country with few independent publishers is that authors, instead of writing what and how they alone can and should write, will choose to write what they suppose one or other of the large conglomerates wants. (A variant of 'I admire your list so much that. . . .') Fewer independent publishers will mean fewer independent writers. Or fewer of them actually getting published.

Publishers need to love books, and to have a sound business sense. Authors customarily have two aspirations: to achieve artistic distinction, and to make money. In today's climate this dichotomy (some would say schizophrenia) appears to have been resolved: literature *is* business, financial success *is* artistic distinction. However, individuals are not always as simple-minded as 'climates'; back in the office, or at the writing-desk, showbiz and razzmatazz soon fade, and old misgivings revive.

A bandwagon is no place for a true writer. Nor for a good, creative publisher, unless it happens to give him a lift to where he really wants to go. Describing him as 'one of the most professional of British publishers' (which goes to show how ambiguous the words 'amateur' and 'professional' are), the *Financial Times* referred to Peter Owen's 'knack of jumping on the right bandwagons'; it needs to be added that he has spotted future bandwagons while they were still stationary and virtually empty. The publication of Hermann Hesse's *Siddhartha* in English, thirty-years after its original appearance, just when the time was ripe for the 'counter-culture' of (modified) Eastern mysticism, must have been due to inspiration, plus egging-on by Henry Miller, rather than calculation. 'Cult' books are not planned, or deliberately resuscitated, they just happen.

In which case inspiration can rise to considerable heights, since by my count Owen has published seven Nobel prizewinners – one, Samuel Beckett, got away because he couldn't afford both Beckett and Osamu Dazai, and picked the latter; at the time either commitment required courage – besides several hot past contenders, and possibly future ones too.

It was through the publication of Dazai's *The Setting Sun* (translated by a friend, Donald Keene), while I was living in Japan, that I first became fully aware of Peter Owen Limited. This and some other notable items, including *Siddhartha*, Yukio Mishima's *Confessions of a Mask*, and two books by Julien Gracq, came Owen's way through a profitable collaboration with the like-minded American publisher, James Laughlin of New Directions, for whom the epithets 'amateur' and 'professional' would be equally apt. Shusaku Endo, whom Owen has published since 1974, and whose sense of religious sin as distinct from social disgrace has commended him to European readers, must be his best-selling Japanese author. In addition to books by Natsume Soseki, my own favourites on the Japanese side of the Peter Owen list are Geoffrey Bownas's translation of Ryūnosuke Akutagawa's satirical story *Kappa* and *The Confessions of Lady Nijō* (translated by Karen Brazell), written around 1307 by a former Imperial concubine; the latter offers much human and some historical interest, without being either prurient or pedantic, and reminds us that as a lively literary medium Japanese prose was not only invented by women but fostered by them. It was later in life that it fell into the hands of men, and became popular, and then disreputable, and then weird.

Colette, Kazantzakis, Pasternak, Pound, Paz, Sartre, Tagore, Apollinaire, Isaac Bashevis Singer, William Carlos Williams, Machado de Assis, Paul Bowles, Cocteau, Giono, Pavese . . . and latterly fiction from Bulgaria, Poland, Latvia, Morocco, Taiwan, Portugal, Holland. . . . Even assuming that Owen forswore the feverish practice of paying out more than could ever be recouped, many of his authors, no matter how celebrated in their native lands, would have given any self-respecting British accountant a fatal seizure. It is not long ago that translated fiction was seen as a sure and swift road to the bankruptcy court.

As well as some of the writers mentioned above, and besides such curiosities as an excerpt from Giorgio de Chirico's painterly novel, the present book features characteristic work by James Purdy, Jane Bowles, Anaïs Nin, Anna Kavan, Cora Sandel, and the highly regarded Norwegian Tarjei Vesaas. All in all, a catalogue of prime exotica, orchids, cacti, monkey-puzzles, sequoias. But Owen has not ignored our native breeds, having published among others Barbara Hardy, Muriel Spark, Robert Liddell, Peter Vansittart, Brian Power, Jeremy Reed.

Presumably Peter Owen is slightly older than Peter Owen Limited. On this fortieth anniversary all their friends and admirers will wish them both many happy returns – including, if one may say so, financial ones. We need them, if only to continue publishing the books richer publishers cannot afford.

PETER OWEN

Books

1952

London

Cover and text page from the first annual book list issued by Peter Owen in 1952

Introduction

I STARTED MY PUBLISHING HOUSE IN 1951, WITH £800 AND A £350 BANK overdraft guaranteed by my mother. (The bank was so distrustful that they required her to give them share certificates as security!) I was very young, enthusiastic and unmarried, so I could live on a pittance. Even in 1951 this was an unrealistic sum with which to start a publishing firm. It was estimated at the time that between £250,000 and £500,000 would be required. I had some experience of most aspects of the work, especially design and production, and was prepared to work hard and alone. Without this ability it would have been impossible, as I could not afford to hire staff. Publishing at that time was more amateur, less competitive and it was easier to sell books, as libraries had more funds and there was less competition from television.

Initially, I was helped by the distinguished American publisher James Laughlin, of New Directions, who let me co-produce some books with his company. The first list consisted of Julien Gracq's surrealist novel *A Dark Stranger*, an anthology of Russian stories, Ezra Pound's *The Spirit of Romance* and Henry Miller's *The Books in My Life*. These were soon followed by Hermann Hesse's *Siddhartha*. James Laughlin and I were advised by Henry Miller, who had good critical taste and vision, that we should acquire Hesse. There existed a translation of this book. Hesse at that time was hardly known outside Germany, although he had recently received the Nobel Prize. No one was particularly interested in him and I secured *Siddhartha* for a £25 advance. Later, in the sixties and seventies, this became our biggest seller, and we published six other books by Hermann Hesse.

It was fun but very hard work. Gradually I had to take on staff as it became impossible for me to do all the editing, design and administration, in addition to typing letters. My first editor was Muriel Spark, who worked for me whilst writing her first novel, *The Comforters*. Muriel was a friend; I had published her book *Emily Brontë*, and a selection of the letters of John Henry Newman compiled by her. She was very efficient and could even do shorthand. She enjoyed the year or so spent as my editor and was considering making publishing her career, but the success of her book prevented this. When Muriel left she was succeeded by the novelist and critic Elizabeth Berridge, who remained with me for several years, until she also left to complete a new book.

The list was growing and the publishing house was being taken seriously. It was making a profit. Among the early books was Boris Pasternak's novel *The Last Summer*. I had bought an anthology in the USA and this short novel was included in it. When Pasternak was awarded the Nobel Prize for *Doctor Zhivago*, I took *The Last Summer* out of the anthology, and it became very successful, going into several printings. Later it was published as a mass-market paperback and I still have it sub-leased to Penguin Books. I also published Isaac Bashevis Singer's *Satan in Goray* and *Gimpel the Fool* around that time. Singer was then unknown and sales of his books were poor. When the small American publisher who had sold him to me sold out to a larger publisher, we could no longer afford to publish him. Later he received the Nobel Prize. Naturally I regretted having lost him – but we were still too small to pay substantial advances for an author with very low sales.

Another of my regrets is having turned down the books of Samuel Beckett, who was at that time also little-known. Muriel Spark wanted me to take him on, but it was a choice between Beckett and the Japanese writer Osamu Dazai – we could not afford both – and I chose Dazai's *The Setting Sun*. A story from *Crackling Mountain* by Dazai, which we recently published, is included in this book.

It has always been my policy to publish books of literary quality. During the 1960s we published Violette Leduc's best-seller *La Bâtarde* and two books by the Guatemalan writer Miguel Angel Asturias, *The Cyclone* and *The Mulatta and Mr Fly*. Soon after publication Asturias was awarded the Nobel Prize. He was *not* one of my favourite people. It was also in the early sixties that I started publishing one of England's most distinguished writers, Peter Vansittart. Since then we have published all of Peter's fiction.

During a holiday in Morocco, my wife Wendy and I discovered that Paul Bowles lived in Tangier. Being admirers of his work, we contacted him. He had just completed a travel book, *Their Heads Are Green*, and he gave me the manuscript to consider. In this way I became his English publisher. I have published all his books, including, of course, *The Sheltering Sky*. For this book I have chosen one of Paul's best stories, 'Pages from Cold Point'. It is taken from the collection of that name which was among the first of Paul's books that I published.

During one of my visits to Paul and his wife Jane, Paul suggested that I publish Jane Bowles's *Two Serious Ladies*, which had appeared only in the USA. I was unfamiliar with her work, and the American edition was very rare. I was able to borrow the book from Ruth Fainlight Sillitoe, who had been given Jane's only copy. I took it on. Wendy read it first and loved it. Later I also published Jane's collection of stories, *Plain Pleasures*, and *The Collected Works of Jane Bowles*. Jane asked me to act for her abroad, which I still do. She has an international following and her books are contemporary classics. I was greatly saddened by her death in 1973.

Paul still lives in Tangier. He misses Jane. He lives an orderly life in the apartment they shared. He is urbane, reserved, and appears more European than American.

GERALD SCARFE'S PEOPLE

including Parliament and Politicians, International Affairs, Berlin, Rest in Peace, People, Egypt, Miscellany, Phantasmagoria, Paris Collections, The Presidential Election 1964, New York, The American Way of Life.

PETER OWEN   London

Title page of *Gerald Scarfe's People*

JUSTICE MUST NOT ONLY BE DONE BUT MUST CLEARLY BE SEEN TO BE DONE

A drawing from *Gerald Scarfe's People*

Other titles published in the sixties included *Gerald Scarfe's People*, and *Ice* by Anna Kavan, which was her breakthrough book when it appeared. I first published Kavan's *Eagles' Nest* in the late 1950s when her early reputation had been forgotten. This was followed by a volume of stories entitled *A Bright Green Field*. Anna kept on reworking the book that became *Ice* until it was almost perfect. She died in 1967 and on the day of her funeral I heard that I had sold the American rights of *Ice*. This would have pleased her. Priscilla Dorr has recently written a full-scale biography of Kavan.

Tarjei Vesaas's *The Ice Palace* was recommended to me by the translator and academic Elizabeth Rokkan. I consider it to be among the best books we have published. Vesaas, a great writer, was a very humble man who regarded his persistent Nobel candidacy with trepidation. When asked during a visit to London whether he would like to receive the award, he replied, 'It would be a great nuisance.' Another major Norwegian writer I publish is Cora Sandel.

One of my most difficult publishing projects was Marc Chagall's early autobiography *My Life*. In the agreement for this book I had given

Chagall the right to approve the translation, believing this to be a formality. The first translation was rejected before it could be edited. I then commissioned other versions which were all rejected. Finally I invoked the arbitration clause in the contract and at the suggestion of Chagall's entourage, Stephen Spender was appointed to read the new translation. He endorsed it and I heard no more from Chagall. The book was published and reprinted. An extract appears in this anthology.

I have published most of Anaïs Nin's books, including the famous *Journals*. Although her early work had gained her a small literary following, she was for years forced to publish her own books. It was in the sixties that she was 'discovered' and adopted by the feminist movement. Her first book, *Under a Glass Bell*, was a collection of stories, one of which is included in this anthology. It was illustrated by her husband Hugo Guyler using his artistic pseudonym Ian Hugo.

On a visit to UNESCO in Paris I was handed a translation of Shusaku Endo's *The Sea and Poison*. Endo at that time was hardly known outside Japan, although his great novel *Silence* had been translated into a number of languages. *The Sea and Poison* appeared in 1974. I soon realized that Endo was a major writer and the first Japanese writer who could be called truly international. I have published all Endo's books, and sell his rights to foreign publishers. As with all really good writers he was at first uncommercial, but is now generally recognized as a great artist. The Endo story that I have included is to some extent autobiographical.

Most writers are nice – some of my authors, for instance Shusaku Endo and Peter Vansittart, are valued friends. The writers who are sometimes difficult are the mediocre people, whose insecurity is vented on their publisher, their agent or the critics.

In the 1970s, the translator and biographer Margaret Crosland, who has often given me good advice, suggested that I publish Salvador Dali's only novel, *Hidden Faces*. I wrote to Dali but received no response. Then, on a visit to Paris, where he was staying, I was invited to the Hôtel Meurice. I thought it was to be a private meeting, but found a noisy, motley crowd courting Dali, who was, however, very pleasant. He suggested I visit him in Cadaqués. He introduced me to Gala, a wizened, cold and rather frightening woman. Before I left Dali said to me, 'Dali loves money.' I was eager to secure the rights of the book and later went to Cadaqués. It was almost impossible to get hotel accommodation there but Dali's manager found me a room. I was invited to the house. Again there was a party of assorted people, including a film producer who was commissioning Dali to design tarot cards for a large fee. Other guests included someone of doubtful sex and a respectable middle-aged woman who was in charge in the absence of Gala. Cheap, sweet Spanish sparkling wine was served by a maid. Dali suggested I return next morning – the guests were disbanded, except for the film producer, who stayed for dinner.

Next day I was shown to a phallic-shaped swimming pool designed by Dali at the rear of the house. The middle-aged woman and another beauty were topless. Dali wore a djellaba. He and his manager were affable and suggested I buy world rights in *Hidden Faces*. They offered some Dali drawings to augment the text and named what was a very large sum. Indeed it was more than I have ever advanced for a book. It was also suggested that Dali would sign a limited edition. I returned once more and found Dali alone. He was entirely businesslike, having talked to Gala, who had reminded him of a snag regarding the American rights (the USA being one of the most important markets). He told me, 'I am a notary's son, and know these things.'

ERTÉ
Things I Remember

An Autobiography

To Peter Owen
with many thanks
for his beautiful
work

London 8-9-75

Peter Owen · London

Title page of *Things I Remember*, Erté. Inscribed to Peter Owen 'with many thanks for his beautiful work' by the author

Full-page illustration from *Things I Remember*, Erté

There was great international interest in this book and rights were sold worldwide. The illustrations, when they arrived, proved disappointing. He should have made more effort. I returned once more, some months later, with my wife, to bring Dali the title pages to be signed for the limited edition. His manager suggested that I paid over some money at this stage to help the process along. When we arrived Dali asked him if I had brought it. Pleased by the reply, he disappeared and changed into a richly embroidered kaftan in our honour. The manager told us to rule pencilled lines on the title pages, as Dali would sign them in bed, and this would keep his signature neat. I suspect this was also where he had drawn the illustrations! When we came to collect the sheets the artist came out to the swimming pool holding a palette. He was gracious and said 'Dali very busy.' Nevertheless he inscribed several books for me and embellished them with drawings of horses.

Erté, whose autobiography *Things I Remember* we published, was charming, modest and very helpful. He was diminutive, slim and spry, although aged over eighty; he wore a mink coat in winter.

Yukio Mishima was a surprising person. I published his key book *Confessions of a Mask* and also his play *Madame de Sade*. I had written some time before that I was visiting Japan, and on my arrival there was a message that he would phone next day to arrange dinner. I was surprised by this efficiency – he told me he had been a civil servant and was trained to cope with detail. He was delightful, spoke good English, and was very sensible. Short, slim yet muscular, he dressed in dark suits. He was being tipped as the Japanese Nobel candidate. I asked him about this and he said it would be awarded to Kawabata, who was the senior Japanese novelist. He was a friend of Kawabata and took me to see him. I met Yukio again in London – Wendy and I both liked him. He had enrolled in a London gymnasium so as not to break his routine of exercise, and on one occasion he offered to take me along. The flamboyant manner of his suicide surprised me because it seemed out of character. He was a very complicated man. I received one of his last letters, handwritten, in English.

In 1970 I published Yoko Ono's *Grapefruit*. My editorial director Beatrice Musgrave and I went to see Yoko at the Apple office. She and John Lennon sat side by side at a large table, wearing identical black, brimmed hats. Lennon did some quick sketches of Yoko, which we used in the book. Yoko, meanwhile, ate caviar with a kitchen spoon from a large Fortnum & Mason jar.

I am one of the few remaining independent publishers. Most publishing houses are now part of conglomerates owned by financiers with no particular interest in literature. Publishing has become more professional but also heartless. Another change that has taken place since I started up is that it is now much harder to sell books. Financiers who run publishing groups cannot adapt to difficult conditions in a civilized and sensible manner. It is my belief that small publishers, if efficiently run, can be more malleable and adjust more easily to adverse trends.

A good publisher or editor requires integrity, acumen and an instinct for literature. It often takes time to establish new writers and to do so costs money, although this may in the end be recouped. Most financiers fail to understand that proper publishing cannot be gauged entirely through an annual balance sheet. My company has always been self-financing and no outside capital has ever been employed. All royalties and bills are paid promptly. I have often found that a really good writer will eventually become profitable.

I intend to remain an independent publisher and to continue discovering good writers from all over the world.

Peter Owen
1991

As Others See Us

'Congratulations on your list which has real quality' – Graham Greene

'Peter Owen is an excellent discoverer of the hidden novels around the world and he encourages them to grow' – Shusaku Endo

'Over the years the list has been consistently a distinguished one' – Paul Bowles

'The independent (some would say maverick) publisher Peter Owen, well known for his persistence in introducing foreign literature to the British public' – *Publishers Weekly*

'Peter Owen is the prince of publishers. In an age of lightning turnovers for writers, and shredding of books of merit, Mr. Owen continues to uphold the great tradition of publishing works of quality and imagination and keeping those works in print in beautiful editions' – James Purdy

'In these days of huge conglomerates in publishing, the survival of Peter Owen as a small, independent and adventurous imprint is a cause for rejoicing. Like the French, the English literary world is a strangely provincial one. To mitigate this provincialism Peter Owen has done more than any other publisher in the postwar years. It has been through translations published by his firm that the English have been enabled to read the works of one of the world's greatest living novelists, Shusaku Endo, and of a host of other first-rate foreign writers' – Francis King

'The only publisher in England who produces anything interesting' – Francis Bacon

'Peter Owen is performing a service making available interesting but often neglected work by European writers' – Julian Symonds, *Sunday Times*

'Dear Peter Owen – how much we owe you! I don't know any house which has taken on so many difficult books to sell and propagate. Blessings!' – Lawrence Durrell

'Peter Owen was the only one who would have taken the risk of publishing the first book of an unknown writer in a remote country [*Cry, the Peacock*]. I marvelled at my luck in finding this small and highly original publishing house' – Anita Desai

'One of a dwindling band of independent publishers who love literature'
– Anthony Curtis, *Financial Times*

'You are one of the few remaining publishers who care about the contents of the books they produce' – Kathleen Raine

'My congratulations to you for bringing out such an unusual, thought-provoking list when all too many publishers are publishing what is merely boring and predictable these days' – Fiona Pitt-Kethley

'You make corporate publishing appear like a graveyard' – Jeremy Reed

'Peter Owen already has the most intelligently selected list of foreign and experimental fiction. We owe him a great deal; he has made the novels of, among others, Asturias, Cendrars, Lengyel and the great Cora Sandel available here' – Martin Seymour-Smith, *The Scotsman*

'Publishing is about the distribution of ideas. It is also an expanding business. It is important that it remains diverse and innovative. Peter Owen fills that bill' – Clive Bradley, Chief Executive, Publishers Association

'Of all the publishing men in my life Peter Owen has been the most constant, the most predictably unpredictable, the most infuriating, the one to whom I always come back' – Margaret Crosland

'Peter Owen has one of the most exotic lists in London publishing' – *Sunday Telegraph*

'Peter Owen is in a special category. By contrast with the large firms and their medium-sized dependants, he is the David whose successful and brilliant career has pioneered a new trend: the emergence of small publishing houses who look for opportunities in the face of the mammoth concerns' – *Frankfurter Allgemeine Zeitung*

'It's always marvellous to publish with Peter Owen. The speed and zest are unequalled. And his list is full of distinction and surprise!' – Barbara Hardy

'These recent translations of foreign novels show that certain go-ahead publishing houses, like Peter Owen, are willing to bring strange and complex works into British book-lists. If the quality of these authors is typical, the exercise is commendable' – *Birmingham Post*

'One of the most professional of British publishers. . . . His knack of jumping on the right bandwagons has ensured that his books are always in demand . . . he has built up a formidable stable of authors' – *Financial Times*

*The following selection
includes the work of some of the best
writers we have published.
Wherever possible, I have chosen
short stories rather than
extracts from novels.*

P.O.

Pages from Cold Point

PAUL BOWLES

Our civilization is doomed to a short life: its component parts are too heterogeneous. I personally am content to see everything in the process of decay. The bigger the bombs, the quicker it will be done. The world is visually too hideous for one to make the attempt to preserve it. Let it go. Perhaps some day another form of life will come along. Either way, it is of no consequence. At the same time, I am still a part of life, and I am bound by this to protect myself to whatever extent I am able. And so I am here. Here in the Islands vegetation still has the upper hand, and man has to fight even to make his presence seen at all. It is beautiful here, the trade winds blow all year, and I suspect that bombs are extremely unlikely to be wasted on this unfrequented side of the island, if indeed on any part of it.

I was loath to give up the house after Hope's death. But it was the obvious move to make. My university career always having been an utter farce (since I believe no reason inducing a man to 'teach' can possibly be a valid one), I was elated by the idea of resigning, and as soon as her affairs had been settled and the money properly invested, I lost no time in doing so.

I think that week was the first time since childhood that I had managed to recapture the feeling of there being a content in existence. I went from one pleasant house to the next, making my adieux to the English quacks, the Philosophy fakirs, and so on – even to those colleagues with whom I was merely on speaking terms. I watched the envy in their faces when I announced my departure by Pan American on Saturday morning; and the greatest pleasure I felt in all this was in being able to answer, 'Nothing', when I was asked, as invariably I was, what I intended to 'do'.

When I was a boy people used to refer to Charles as 'Big Brother C.', although he is only a scant year older than I. To me now he is merely 'Fat Brother C.', a successful lawyer. His thick red face and hands, his back-slapping joviality, and his fathomless hypocritical prudery, these are the qualities which make him truly repulsive to me. There is also the fact that he once looked not unlike the way Racky does now. And after all, he is still my big brother, and disapproves openly of everything I do. The loathing I feel for him is so strong that for years I have not been able to swallow a morsel of food or a drop of liquid in his presence without making a prodigious effort. No one knows this but me – certainly not Charles, who would be the last one I should tell about it. He came up on the late train two nights before I left. He got quickly to the point – as soon as he was settled with a highball.

'So you're off for the wilds,' he said, sitting forward in his chair like a salesman.

'If you can call it the wilds,' I replied. 'Certainly it's not wild like Mitichi.' (He has a lodge in northern Quebec.) 'I consider it really civilized.'

He drank and smacked his lips together stiffly, bringing the glass down hard on his knee.

'And Racky. You're taking him along?'

'Of course.'

'Out of school. Away. So he'll see nobody but you. You think that's good.'

I looked at him. 'I do,' I said.

'By God, if I could stop you legally, I would!' he cried, jumping up and putting his glass on the mantel. I was trembling inwardly with excitement, but I merely sat and watched him. He went on. 'You're not fit to have custody of the kid!' he shouted. He shot a stern glance at me over his spectacles.

'You think not?' I said gently.

Again he looked sharply at me. 'D'ye think I've forgotten?'

I was understandably eager to get him out of the house as soon as I could. As I piled and sorted letters and magazines on the desk, I said: 'Is that all you came to tell me? I have a good deal to do tomorrow and I must get some sleep. I probably shan't see you at breakfast. Agnes'll see that you eat in time to make the early train.'

All he said was: 'God! Wake up! Get wise to yourself! You're not fooling anybody, you know.'

That kind of talk is typical of Charles. His mind is slow and obtuse; he constantly imagines that everyone he meets is playing some private game of deception with him. He is so utterly incapable of following the functioning of even a moderately evolved intellect that he finds the will to secretiveness and duplicity everywhere.

'I haven't time to listen to that sort of nonsense,' I said, preparing to leave the room.

But he shouted: 'You don't want to listen! No! Of course not! You just want to do what you want to do. You just want to go on off down there and live as you've a mind to, and to hell with the consequences!' At this point I heard Racky coming downstairs. C. obviously heard nothing, and he raved on. 'But just remember, I've got your number all right, and if there's any trouble with the boy I'll know who's to blame.'

I hurried across the room and opened the door so he could see that Racky was there in the hallway. That stopped his tirade. It was hard to know whether Racky had heard any of it or not. Although he is not a quiet young person, he is the soul of discretion, and it is almost never possible to know any more about what goes on inside his head than he intends one to know.

I was annoyed that C. should have been bellowing at me in my own house. To be sure, he is the only one from whom I would accept such behavior, but then, no father likes to have his son see him take criticism meekly. Racky simply stood there in his bathrobe, his angelic face quite devoid of expression, saying: 'Tell Uncle Charley good night for me, will you? I forgot.'

I said I would, and quickly shut the door. When I thought Racky was back upstairs in his room, I bade Charles good night. I have never been able to get out of his presence fast enough. The effect he has on me dates from an early period of our lives, from days I dislike to recall.

Racky is a wonderful boy. After we arrived, when we found it impossible to secure a proper house near any town where he might have the company of English boys and girls his own age, he showed no sign of chagrin, although he must have been disappointed. Instead, as we went out of the renting office into the glare of the street, he grinned and said: 'Well, I guess we'll have to get bikes, that's all.'

The few available houses near what Charles would have called 'civilization' turned out to be so ugly and so impossibly confining in atmosphere that we decided immediately on Cold Point, even though it was across the island and quite isolated on its seaside cliff. It was beyond a doubt one of the most desirable properties on the island, and Racky was as enthusiastic about its splendors as I.

'You'll get tired of being alone out there, just with me,' I said to him as we walked back to the hotel.

'Aw, I'll get along all right. When do we look for the bikes?'

At his insistence we bought two the next morning. I was sure I should not make much use of mine, but I reflected that an extra bicycle might be convenient to have around the house. It turned out that all the servants had their own bicycles, without which they would not have been able to get to and from the village of Orange Walk, eight miles down the shore. So for a while I was forced to get astride mine each morning before breakfast and pedal madly along beside Racky for a half-hour. We would ride through the cool early air, under the towering silk-cotton trees near the house, and out to the great curve in the shoreline where the waving palms bend landward in the stiff breeze that always blows there. Then we would make a wide turn and race back to the house, loudly discussing the degrees of our desires for the various items of breakfast we knew were awaiting us there on the terrace. Back home we would eat in the wind, looking out over the Caribbean, and talk about the news in yesterday's local paper, brought to us by Isiah each morning from Orange Walk. Then Racky would disappear for the whole morning on his bicycle, riding furiously along the road in one direction or the other until he had discovered an unfamiliar strip of sand along the shore that he could consider a new beach. At lunch he would describe it in detail to me, along with a recounting of all the physical hazards involved in hiding the bicycle among the trees (so that natives passing along the road on foot would not spot it), or in climbing down unscalable cliffs that turned out to be much higher than they had appeared at first sight, or in measuring the depth of the water preparatory to diving from the rocks, or in judging the efficacy of the reef in barring sharks and barracuda.

There is never any element of braggadocio in Racky's relating of his exploits – only the joyous excitement he derives from telling how he satisfies his inexhaustible curiosity. And his mind shows its alertness in all directions at once. I do not mean to say that I expect him to be an 'intellectual'. That is no affair of mine, nor do I have any particular interest in whether or not he turns out to be a thinking man. I know he will always have a certain boldness of manner and a great purity of spirit in judging values. The former will prevent his becoming what I call a 'victim': he never will be brutalized by realities. And his unerring sense of balance in ethical considerations will shield him from the paralyzing effects of present-day materialism.

For a boy of sixteen Racky has an extraordinary inno-cence of vision. I do not say that as a doting father, although God knows I can never even think of the boy without that familiar overwhelming sensation of delight and gratitude for being vouchsafed the privilege of sharing my life with him. What he takes so completely as a matter of course, our daily life here together, is a source of never-ending wonder to me; and I reflect upon it a good part of each day, just sitting here being conscious of my great good fortune in having him all to myself, beyond the reach of prying eyes and malicious tongues. (I suppose I am really thinking of C. when I write that.) And I believe that a part of the charm in sharing Racky's life with him consists precisely in his taking it all so utterly for granted. I have never asked him whether he likes being here – it is so patent that he does, very much. I think if he were to turn to me one day and tell me how happy he is here, that somehow, perhaps, the spell might be broken. Yet if he were to be thoughtless and inconsiderate, or even unkind to me, I feel that I should be able only to love him the more for it.

I have reread that last sentence. What does it mean? And why should I even imagine it could mean anything more than it says?

Still, much as I may try, I can never believe in the gratuitous, isolated fact. What I must mean is that I feel that Racky already has been in some way inconsiderate. But in what way? Surely I cannot resent his bicycle treks; I cannot expect him to want to stay and sit talking with me all day. And I never worry about his being in danger; I know he is more capable than most adults of taking care of himself, and that he is no more likely than any native to come to harm crawling over the cliffs or swimming in the bays. At the same time there is no doubt in my mind that something about our existence annoys me. I must resent some detail in the pattern, whatever that pattern may be. Perhaps it is just his youth, and I am envious of the lithe body, the smooth skin, the animal energy and grace.

For a long time this morning I sat looking out to sea, trying to solve that small puzzle. Two white herons came and perched on a dead stump, east of the garden. They stayed a long time there without stirring. I would turn my head away and accustom my eyes to the bright sea-horizon, then I would look suddenly at them to see if they had shifted position, but they would always be in the same attitude. I tried to imagine the black stump without them – a purely vegetable landscape – but it was impossible. All the while I was slowly forcing myself to accept a ridiculous explanation of my annoyance with Racky. It had made itself manifest to me only yesterday, when instead of appearing for lunch, he had sent a young colored boy from Orange Walk to say that he would be lunching in the village. I could not help noticing that the boy was riding Racky's bicycle. I had been waiting lunch a good half-hour for him, and I had Gloria serve immediately as the boy rode off, back to the village. I was curious to know in what sort of place and with whom Racky could be eating, since Orange Walk, as far as I know, is inhabited exclusively by Negroes, and I was sure Gloria would be able to shed some light on the matter, but I could scarcely ask her. However, as she brought on the dessert, I said: 'Who was that boy that brought the message from Mister Racky?'

She shrugged her shoulders. 'A young lad of Orange Walk. He's named Wilmot.'

When Racky returned at dusk, flushed from his exertion (for he never rides casually), I watched him closely. His behavior struck my already suspicious eyes as being one of false heartiness and a rather forced good humor. He went to his room early and read for quite a while before turning off his light. I took a long walk in the almost day-bright moonlight, listening to the songs of the night insects in the trees. And I sat for a while in the dark on the stone railing of the bridge across Black River. (It is really only a brook that rushes down over the rocks from the mountain a few miles inland, to the beach near the house.) In the night it always sounds louder and more important than it does in the daytime. The music of the water over the stones relaxed my nerves, although why I had need of such a thing I find it difficult to understand, unless I was really upset by Racky's not having come home to lunch. But if that were true it would be absurd, and moreover, dangerous – just the sort of thing the parent of an adolescent has to beware of and fight against, unless he is indifferent to the prospect of losing the trust and affection of his offspring permanently. Racky must stay out whenever he likes, with whom he likes, and for as long as he likes, and I must not think twice about it, much less mention it to him, or in any way give the impression of prying. Lack of confidence on the part of a parent is the one unforgivable sin.

Although we still take our morning dip together on arising, it is three weeks since we have been for the early spin. One morning I found that Racky had jumped onto his bicycle in his wet trunks while I was still swimming, and gone by himself, and since then there has been an unspoken agreement between us that such is to be the procedure: he will go alone. Perhaps I held him back; he likes to ride so fast.

Young Peter, the smiling gardener from Saint Ives Cove, is Racky's special friend. It is amusing to see them together among the bushes, crouched over an ant-hill or rushing about trying to catch a lizard, almost of an age the two, yet so disparate – Racky with his tan skin looking nearly white in contrast to the glistening black of the other. Today I know I shall be alone for lunch, since it is Peter's day off. On such days they usually go together on their bicycles into Saint Ives Cove, where Peter keeps a small rowboat. They fish along the coast there, but they have never returned with anything so far.

Meanwhile I am here alone, sitting on the rocks in the sun, from time to time climbing down to cool myself in the water, always conscious of the house behind me under the high palms, like a large glass boat filled with orchids and lilies. The servants are clean and quiet, and the work seems to be accomplished almost automatically. The good, black servants are another blessing of the Islands; the British, born here in this paradise, have no conception of how fortunate they are. In fact, they do nothing but complain. One must have lived in the United States to appreciate the wonder of this place. Still, even here ideas are changing each day. Soon the people will decide that they want their land to be a part of today's monstrous world, and once that happens, it will be all over. As soon as you have that desire, you are infected with the deadly virus, and you begin to show the symptoms of the disease. You live in terms of time and money, and you think in terms of society and progress. Then all that is left for you is to kill the other people who think the same way, along with a good many of those who do not, since that is the final manifestation of the malady. Here for the moment at any rate, one has a feeling of staticity – existence ceases to be like those last few seconds in the hourglass when what is left of the sand suddenly begins to rush through to the bottom all at once. For the moment, it seems suspended. And if it seems, it is. Each wave at my feet, each bird-call in the forest at my back, does *not* carry me one step nearer the final disaster. The disaster is certain, but it will suddenly have happened, that is all. Until then, time stays still.

I am upset by a letter in this morning's mail: the Royal Bank of Canada requests that I call in person at its central office to sign the deposit slips and other papers for a sum that was cabled from the bank in Boston. Since the central office is on the other side of the island, fifty miles away, I shall have to spend the night over there and return the following day. There is no point in taking Racky along. The sight of 'civilization' might awaken a longing for it in him; one never knows. I am sure it would have done in me when I was his age. And if that should once start, he would merely be unhappy, since there is nothing for him but to stay here with me, at least for the next two years, when I hope to renew the lease, or, if things in New York pick up, buy the place. I am sending word by Isiah, when he goes home into Orange Walk this evening, to have the McCoigh car call for me at seven-thirty tomorrow morning. It is an enormous old open Packard, and Isiah can save the ride out to work here by piling his bicycle into the back and riding with McCoigh.

The trip across the island was beautiful, and would have been highly enjoyable if my imagination had not played me a strange trick at the very outset. We stopped in Orange Walk for gasoline, and while that was being seen to, I got out and went to the corner store for some cigarettes. Since it was not yet eight o'clock, the store was still closed, and I hurried up the side street to the other little shop which I thought might be open. It was, and I bought my cigarettes. On the way back to the corner I noticed a large black woman leaning with her arms on the gate in front of her tiny house, staring into the street. As I passed by her, she looked straight into my face and said something with the strange accent of the island. It was said in what seemed an unfriendly tone, and ostensibly was directed at me, but I had no notion of what it was. I got back into the car and the driver started it. The sound of the words had stayed in my head, however, as a bright shape outlined by darkness is likely to stay in the mind's eye, in such a way that when one shuts one's eyes one can see the exact contour of the shape. The car was already roaring up the hill toward the overland road when I suddenly reheard the very words. And they were: 'Keep your boy at home, mahn.' I sat perfectly rigid for a moment as the open countryside rushed past. Why should I think she had said that? Immediately I decided that I was giving an arbitrary sense to a phrase I could not have understood even if I had been paying strict attention. And then I wondered why my subconscious should have chosen that sense, since now that I whispered the words over to myself they failed to connect with any anxiety to which my mind might have been disposed. Actually I have never given a thought to Racky's wanderings about Orange Walk. I can find no such preoccupation no matter how I put the question to myself. Then, could she really have said those words? All the way through the mountains I pondered the question, even though it was obviously a waste of energy. And soon I could no longer hear the sound of her voice in my memory: I had played the record over too many times, and worn it out.

Here in the hotel, a gala dance is in progress. The abominable orchestra, comprising two saxophones and one sour violin, is playing directly under my window in the garden, and the serious-looking couples slide about on the waxed concrete floor of the terrace, in the light of strings of paper lanterns. I suppose it is meant to look Japanese.

At this moment I wonder what Racky is doing there in the house with only Peter and Ernest the watchman to keep him company. I wonder if he is asleep. The house, which I am accustomed to think of as smiling and benevolent in its airiness, could just as well be in the most sinister and remote regions of the globe, now that I am here. Sitting with the absurd orchestra bleating downstairs, I picture it to myself, and it strikes me as terribly vulnerable in its isolation. In my mind's eye I see the moonlit point with its tall palms waving restlessly in the wind, its dark cliffs licked by the waves below. Suddenly, although I struggle against the sensation, I am inexpressibly glad to be away from the house, helpless there, far on its point of land, in the silence of the night. Then I remember that the night is seldom silent. There are the occasional cries of the night birds, the droning of the thousands of insects, the loud sea at the base of the rocks – all the familiar noises that make sleep so sound. And Racky is there surrounded by them as usual, not even hearing them. But I feel profoundly guilty for having left him, unutterably tender and sad at the thought of him, lying there alone in the house with the two Negroes the only human beings within miles. If I keep thinking of Cold Point I shall be more and more nervous.

I am not going to bed yet. They are all screaming with laughter down there, the idiots; I could never sleep anyway. The bar is still open. Fortunately it is on the street side of the hotel. For once I need a few drinks.

Much later, but I feel no better; I may be a little drunk. The dance is over and it is quiet in the garden, but the room is too hot.

As I was falling asleep last night, all dressed, and with the overhead light shining sordidly in my face, I heard the black woman's voice again, more clearly even than I did in the car yesterday. For some reason this morning there is no doubt in my mind that the words I heard are the words she said. I accept that and go on from there. Suppose she did tell me to keep Racky home. It could only mean that she, or someone else in Orange Walk, has had a childish altercation with him; although I must say it is hard to conceive of Racky's entering into any sort of argument or feud with those people. To set my mind at rest (for I do seem to be taking the whole thing with great seriousness), I am going to stop in the village this afternoon before going home, and try to see the woman. I am extremely curious to know what she could have meant.

I had not been conscious until this evening when I came back to Cold Point how powerful they are, all those physical elements that go to make up its atmosphere: the sea and wind sounds that isolate the house from the road, the brilliancy of the water, sky and sun, the bright colors and strong odors of the flowers, the feeling of space both outside and within the house. One naturally accepts these things when one is living here. This afternoon when I returned I was conscious of them all over again, of their existence and their strength. All of them together are like a powerful drug; coming back made me feel as though I had been disintoxicated and were returning to the scene of my former indulgences. Now at eleven it is as if I had never been absent an hour. Everything is the same as always, even to the dry palm branch that scrapes against the window screen by my night table. And indeed, it is only thirty-six hours since I was here; but I always expect my absence from a place to bring about irremediable changes.

Strangely enough, now that I think of it, I feel that something *has* changed since I left yesterday morning, and that is the general attitude of the servants – their collective aura, so to speak. I noticed that difference immediately upon arriving back, but was unable to define it. Now I see it clearly. The network of common understanding which slowly spreads itself through a well-run household has been destroyed. Each person is by himself now. No unfriendliness, however, that I can see. They all behave with the utmost courtesy, excepting possibly Peter, who struck me as looking unaccustomedly glum when I encountered him in the kitchen after dinner. I meant to ask Racky if he had noticed it, but I forgot, and he went to bed early.

In Orange Walk I made a brief stop, on the pretext to McCoigh that I wanted to see the seamstress in the side street. I walked up and back in front of the house where I had seen the woman, but there was no sign of anyone.

As for my absence, Racky seems to have been perfectly content, having spent most of the day swimming off the rocks below the terrace. The insect sounds are at their height now, the breeze is cooler than usual, and I shall take advantage of these favorable conditions to get a good long night's rest.

Today has been one of the most difficult days of my life. I arose early, we had breakfast at the regular time, and Racky went off in the direction of Saint Ives Cove. I lay in the sun on the terrace for a while, listening to the noises of the household's regime. Peter was all over the property, collecting dead leaves and fallen blossoms in a huge basket, and carrying them off to the compost heap. He appeared to be in an even fouler humor than last night. When he came near to me at one point, on his way down to another part of the garden, I called to him. He set the basket down and stood looking at me; then he walked across the grass toward me slowly – reluctantly, it seemed to me.

'Peter, is everything all right with you?'

'Yes, sir.'

'No trouble at home?'

'Oh, no, sir.'

'Good.'

'Yes, sir.'

He went back to his work. But his face belied his words. Not only did he seem to be in a decidedly unpleasant temper; out here in the sunlight he looked positively ill. However, it was not my concern, if he refused to admit it.

When the heavy heat of the sun reached the unbearable point for me, I got out of my chair and went down the side of the cliff along the series of steps cut there in the rock. A level platform is below, and a diving board, for the water is deep. At each side, the rocks spread out and the waves break over them, but by the platform the wall of rock is vertical and the water merely hits against it below the springboard. The place is a tiny amphitheater, quite cut off in sound and sight from the house. There too, I like to lie in the sun; when I climb out of the water I often remove my trunks and lie stark naked on the springboard. I regularly make fun of Racky because he is embarrassed to do the same. Occasionally he will do it, but never without being coaxed. I was spread out there without a stitch on, being lulled by the slapping of the water, when an unfamiliar voice very close to me said: 'Mister Norton?'

I jumped with nervousness, nearly fell off the springboard, and sat up, reaching at the same time, but in vain, for my trunks, which were lying on the rock practically at the feet of a middle-aged mulatto gentleman. He was in a white duck suit, and wore a high collar with a black tie, and it seemed to me that he was eyeing me with a certain degree of horror.

My next reaction was one of anger at being trespassed upon in this way. I rose and got the trunks, however, donning them calmly and saying nothing more meaningful than: 'I didn't hear you come down the steps.'

'Shall we go up?' said my caller. As he led the way, I had

a definite premonition that he was here on an unpleasant errand. On the terrace we sat down, and he offered me an American cigarette which I did not accept.

'This is a delightful spot,' he said, glancing out to sea and then at the end of his cigarette, which was only partially aglow. He puffed at it.

I said: 'Yes,' waiting for him to go on; presently he did.

'I am from the constabulary of this parish. The police, you see.' And seeing my face, 'This is a friendly call. But still it must be taken as a warning, Mister Norton. It is very serious. If anyone else comes to you about this it will mean trouble for you, heavy trouble. That's why I want to see you privately this way and warn you personally. You see.'

I could not believe I was hearing his words. At length I said faintly: 'But what about?'

'This is not an official call. You must not be upset. I have taken it upon myself to speak to you because I want to save you deep trouble.'

'But I *am* upset!' I cried, finding my voice at last. 'How can I help being upset, when I don't know what you're talking about?'

He moved his chair closer to mine, and spoke in a very low voice.

'I have waited until the young man was away from the house so we could talk in private. You see, it is about him.'

Somehow that did not surprise me. I nodded.

'I will tell you very briefly. The people here are simple country folk. They make trouble easily. Right now they are all talking about the young man you have living here with you. He is your son, I hear.' His inflection here was skeptical.

'Certainly he's my son.'

His expression did not change, but his voice grew indignant. 'Whoever he is, that is a bad young man.'

'What do you mean?' I cried, but he cut in hotly: 'He may be your son; he may not be. I don't care who he is. That is not my affair. But he is bad through and through. We don't have such things going on here, sir. The people in Orange

41

Walk and Saint Ives Cove are very cross now. You don't know what these folk do when they are aroused.'

I thought it my turn to interrupt. 'Please tell me why you say my son is bad. What has he done?' Perhaps the earnestness in my voice reached him, for his face assumed a gentler aspect. He leaned still closer to me and almost whispered.

'He has no shame. He does what he pleases with all the young boys, and the men too, and gives them a shilling so they won't tell about it. But they talk. Of course they talk. Every man for twenty miles up and down the coast knows about it. And the women too, they know about it.' There was a silence.

I had felt myself preparing to get to my feet for the past few seconds because I wanted to go into my room and be alone, to get away from that scandalized stage whisper. I think I mumbled 'Good morning' or 'Thank you' as I turned away and began walking toward the house. But he was still beside me, still whispering like an eager conspirator into my ear: 'Keep him home, Mister Norton. Or send him away to school, if he is your son. But make him stay out of these towns. For his own sake.'

I shook hands with him and went to lie on my bed. From there I heard his car door slam, heard him drive off. I was painfully trying to formulate an opening sentence to use in speaking to Racky about this, feeling that the opening sentence would define my stand. The attempt was merely a sort of therapeutic action, to avoid thinking about the thing itself. Every attitude seemed impossible. There was no way to broach the subject. I suddenly realized that I should never be able to speak to him directly about it. With the advent of this news he had become another person – an adult, mysterious and formidable. To be sure, it did occur to me that the mulatto's story might not be true, but automatically I rejected the doubt. It was as if I wanted to believe it, almost as if I had already known it, and he had merely confirmed it.

Racky returned at midday, panting and grinning. The inevitable comb appeared and was used on the sweaty, unruly locks. Sitting down to lunch, he exclaimed: 'Wow! What a beach I found this morning! But what a job to get down to it!' I tried to look unconcerned as I met his gaze; it was as if our positions had been reversed, and I were hoping to stem his rebuke. He prattled on about thorns and vines and his machete. Throughout the meal I kept telling myself: 'Now is the moment. You must say something.' But all I said was: 'More salad? Or do you want dessert now?' So the lunch passed and nothing happened. After I had finished my coffee I went into my bedroom and looked at myself in the large mirror. I saw my eyes trying to give their reflected brothers a little courage. As I stood there I heard a commotion in the other wing of the house: voices, bumpings, the sound of a scuffle. Above the noise came Gloria's sharp voice, imperious and excited: 'No, mahn! Don't strike him!' And louder: 'Peter, mahn, no!'

I went quickly toward the kitchen, where the trouble seemed to be, but on the way I was run into by Racky, who staggered into the hallway with his hands in front of his face.

'What is it, Racky?' I cried.

He pushed past me into the living room without moving his hands away from his face; I turned and followed him. From there he went into his own room, leaving the door open behind him. I heard him in the bathroom running the water. I was undecided what to do. Suddenly Peter appeared in the hall doorway, his hat in his hand. When he raised his head, I was surprised to see that his cheek was bleeding. In his eyes was a strange, confused expression of transient fear and deep hostility. He looked down again.

'May I please talk with you, sir?'

'What was all the racket? What's been happening?'

'May I talk with you outside, sir?' He said it doggedly, still not looking up.

In view of the circumstances, I humored him. We walked slowly up the cinder road to the main highway, across the bridge, and through the forest while he told me his story. I said nothing.

At the end he said: 'I never wanted to, sir, even the first time, but after the first time I was afraid, and Mister Racky was after me every day.'

I stood still, and finally said: 'If you had only told me this the first time it happened, it would have been much better for everyone.'

He turned his hat in his hands, studying it intently. 'Yes, sir. But I didn't know what everyone was saying about him in Orange Walk until today. You know I always go to the beach at Saint Ives Cove with Mister Racky on my free days. If I had known what they were all saying I wouldn't have been afraid, sir. And I wanted to keep on working here. I needed the money.' Then he repeated what he had already said three times. 'Mister Racky said you'd see about it that I was put in the jail. I'm a year older than Mister Racky, sir.'

'I know, I know,' I said impatiently; and deciding that severity was what Peter expected of me at this point I added: 'You had better get your things together and go home. You can't work here any longer, you know.'

The hostility in his face assumed terrifying proportions as he said: 'If you killed me I would not work any more at Cold Point, sir.'

I turned and walked briskly back to the house, leaving him standing there in the road. It seems he returned at dusk, a little while ago, and got his belongings.

In his room Racky was reading. He had stuck some adhesive tape on his chin and over his cheekbone.

'I've dismissed Peter,' I announced. 'He hit you, didn't he?'

He glanced up. His left eye was swollen, but not yet black.

'He sure did. But I landed him one, too. And I guess I deserved it anyway.'

I rested against the table. 'Why?' I asked nonchalantly.

'Oh, I had something on him from a long time back that he was afraid I'd tell you.'

'And just now you threatened to tell me?'

'Oh, no! He said he was going to quit the job here, and I told him he was yellow.'

'Why did he want to quit? I thought he liked the job.'

'Well, he did, I guess, but he didn't like me.' Racky's candid gaze betrayed a shade of pique. I still leaned against the table.

I persisted. 'But I thought you two got on fine together. You seemed to.'

'Nah. He was just scared of losing his job. I had something on him. He was a good guy, though. I liked him all right.' He paused. 'Has he gone yet?' A strange quaver crept into his voice as he said the last words, and I understood that for the first time Racky's heretofore impeccable histrionics were not quite equal to the occasion. He was very much upset at losing Peter.

'Yes, he's gone,' I said shortly. 'He's not coming back, either.' And as Racky, hearing the unaccustomed inflection in my voice, looked up at me suddenly with faint astonishment in his young eyes, I realized that this was the moment to press on, to say: 'What did you have on him?' But as if he had arrived at the same spot in my mind a fraction of a second earlier, he proceeded to snatch away my advantage by jumping up, bursting into loud song, and pulling off all his clothes. As he stood before me naked, singing at the top of his lungs, and stepped into his swimming trunks, I was conscious that again I should be incapable of saying to him what I must say.

He was in and out of the house all afternoon: some of the time he read in his room, and most of the time he was down on the diving board. It is strange behavior for him; if I could only know what is in his mind. As evening approached, my problem took on a purely obsessive-character. I walked to and fro in my room, always pausing at one end to look out the window over the sea, and at the other end to glance at my face in the mirror. As if that could help me! Then I took a drink. And another. I thought I might be able to do it at dinner, when I felt fortified by the whiskey. But no. Soon he will have gone to bed. It is not that I expect to confront him with any accusations. That I know I never can do. But I must find a way to keep him from his wanderings, and I must invent a reason to give him, so that he will never suspect that I know.

We fear for the future of our offspring. It is ludicrous, but only a little more palpably so than most things in life. A length of time has passed – days which I am content to have known, even if now they are over. I think that this period was what I had always been waiting for life to offer, the recompense I had unconsciously but firmly expected, in return for having been held so closely in the grip of existence all these years.

That evening seems long ago only because I have re-called its details so many times that they have taken on the color of legend. Actually my problem already had been solved for me then, but I did not know it. Because I could not perceive the pattern, I foolishly imagined that I must cudgel my brains to find the right words with which to approach Racky. But it was he who came to me. That same evening, as I was about to go out for a solitary stroll which I thought might help me hit upon a formula, he appeared at my door.

'Going for a walk?' he asked, seeing the stick in my hand.

The prospect of making an exit immediately after speak-ing with him made things seem simpler. 'Yes,' I said, 'but I'd like to have a word with you first.'

'Sure. What?' I did not look at him because I did not want to see the watchful light I was sure was playing in his eyes at this moment. As I spoke I tapped with my stick along the designs made by the tiles in the floor. 'Racky, would you like to go back to school?'

'Are you kidding? You know I hate school.'

I glanced up at him. 'No, I'm not kidding. Don't look so horrified. You'd probably enjoy being with a bunch of fellows your own age.' (That was not one of the arguments I had meant to use.)

'I might like to be with guys my own age, but I don't want to have to be in school to do it. I've had school enough.'

I went to the door and said lamely: 'I thought I'd get your reactions.'

He laughed, 'No, thanks.'

'That doesn't mean you're not going,' I said over my shoulder as I went out.

On my walk I pounded the highway's asphalt with my stick, stood on the bridge having dramatic visions which involved such eventualities as our moving back to the States, Racky's having a bad spill on his bicycle and being paralyzed for some months, and even the possibility of my letting events take their course, which would doubtless mean my having to visit him now and then in the governmental prison with gifts of food, if it meant nothing more tragic and violent. 'But none of these things will happen,' I said to myself, and I knew I was wasting precious time; he must not return to Orange Walk tomorrow.

I went back toward the point at a snail's pace. There was no moon, and very little breeze. As I approached the house, trying to tread lightly on the cinders so as not to awaken the watchful Ernest and have to explain to him that it was only I, I saw that there were no lights in Racky's room. The house was dark save for the dim lamp on my night table. Instead of going in, I skirted the entire building, colliding with bushes and getting my face sticky with spider webs, and went to sit a while on the terrace where there seemed to be a breath of air. The sound of the sea was far out on the reef, where the breakers sighed. Here below, there were only slight watery chugs and gurgles now and then. It was an unusually low tide. I smoked three cigarettes mechanically, having ceased even to think, and then, my mouth tasting bitter from the smoke, I went inside.

My room was airless. I flung my clothes onto a chair and looked at the night table to see if the carafe of water was there. Then my mouth opened. The top sheet of my bed had been stripped back to the foot. There on the far side of the bed, dark against the whiteness of the lower sheet, lay Racky asleep on his side, and naked.

I stood looking at him for a long time, probably holding my breath, for I remember feeling a little dizzy at one point. I was whispering to myself, as my eyes followed the curve of his arm, shoulder, back, thigh, leg: 'A child. A child.' Destiny, when one perceives it clearly from very near, has no qualities at all. The recognition of it and the consciousness of the vision's clarity leave no room on the mind's horizon. Finally I turned off the light and softly lay down. The night was absolutely black.

He stayed perfectly quiet until dawn. I shall never know whether or not he was really asleep all that time. Of course he couldn't have been, and yet he lay so still. Warm and firm, but still as death. The darkness and silence were heavy around us. As the birds began to sing, I sank into a soft, enveloping slumber; when I awoke in the sunlight later, he was gone.

I found him down by the water, cavorting alone on the springboard; for the first time, he had discarded his trunks without my suggesting it. All day we stayed together around the terrace and on the rocks, talking, swimming, reading, and just lying flat in the hot sun. Nor did he return to his room when night came. Instead, after the servants were asleep, we brought three bottles of champagne in and set the pail on the night table.

Thus it came about that I was able to touch on the delicate subject that still preoccupied me, and profiting by the new understanding between us, I made my request in the easiest, most natural fashion.

'Racky, would you do me a tremendous favor if I asked you?'

He lay on his back, his hands beneath his head. It seemed to me his regard was circumspect, wanting in candor.

'I guess so,' he said. 'What is it?'

'Will you stay around the house for a few days – a week, say? Just to please me? We can take some rides together, as far as you like. Would you do that for me?'

'Sure thing,' he said, smiling.

I was temporizing, but I was desperate.

Perhaps a week later (it is only when one is not fully happy that one is meticulous about time, so that it may have been more, or less) we were having breakfast. Isiah stood by in the shade, waiting to pour us more coffee.

'I noticed you had a letter from Uncle Charley the other day,' said Racky. 'Don't you think we ought to invite him down?'

My heart began to beat with great force.

'Here? He'd hate it here,' I said casually. 'Besides, there's no room. Where would he sleep?' Even as I heard myself saying the words, I knew that they were the wrong ones, and that I was not really participating in the conversation. Again I felt the fascination of complete helplessness that comes when one is suddenly a conscious onlooker at the shaping of one's fate.

'In my room,' said Racky. 'It's empty.'

I could see more of the pattern at that moment than I had ever suspected existed. 'Nonsense,' I said. 'This is not the sort of place for Uncle Charley.'

Racky appeared to be hitting on an excellent idea. 'Maybe if I wrote and invited him,' he suggested, motioning to Isiah for more coffee.

'Nonsense,' I said again, watching still more of the pattern reveal itself, like a photographic print becoming constantly clearer in a tray of developing solution.

Isiah filled Racky's cup and returned to the shade. Racky drank slowly, pretending to be savoring the coffee.

'Well, it won't do any harm to try. He'd appreciate the invitation,' he said speculatively.

For some reason, at this juncture I knew what to say, and as I said it, I knew what I was going to do.

'I thought we might fly over to Havana for a few days next week.'

He looked guardedly interested, and then he broke into a wide grin. 'Great!' he cried. 'Why wait until next week?'

The next morning the servants called 'Good-bye' to us as we drove up the cinder road in the McCoigh car. We took off from the airport at six that evening. Racky was in high spirits; he kept the stewardess engaged in conversation all the way to Camagüey.

He was delighted with Havana. Sitting in the bar at the Nacional, we continued to discuss the possibility of having C. pay us a visit at the island. It was not without difficulty that I eventually managed to persuade Racky that writing him would be inadvisable.

We decided to look for an apartment right there in Vedado for Racky. He did not seem to want to come back to Cold Point. We also decided that living in Havana he would need a larger income than I. I am already having the greater part of Hope's estate transferred to his name in the form of a trust fund which I shall administer until he is of age. It was his mother's money, after all.

We bought a new convertible, and he drove me out to Rancho Boyeros in it when I took my plane. A Cuban named Claudio with very white teeth, whom Racky had met in the pool that morning, sat between us.

We were waiting in front of the landing field. An official finally unhooked the chain to let the passengers through. 'If you get fed up, come to Havana,' said Racky, pinching my arm.

The two of them stood together behind the rope, waving to me, their shirts flapping in the wind as the plane started to move.

The wind blows by my head; between each wave there are thousands of tiny licking and chopping sounds as the water hurries out of the crevices and holes; and a part-floating, part-submerged feeling of being in the water haunts my mind even as the hot sun burns my face. I sit here and I read, and I wait for the pleasant sensation of repletion that follows a good meal, to turn slowly, as the hours pass along, into the even more delightful, slightly stirring emotion deep within, which accompanies the awakening of the appetite.

I am perfectly happy here in reality, because I believe that nothing very drastic is likely to befall this part of the island in the near future.

Title story from the collection *Pages from Cold Point*

The drawings on this and the following page are by Denton Welch; used as decorative tailpieces in *Poetry London*, Volume 2 Number 9, they are reproduced here slightly larger than in the original. © Poetry London [1943].

A page from *Tambimuttu: Bridge Between Two Worlds*, edited by Jane Williams

A Forty-Year-Old Man

SHUSAKU ENDO

1

People sometimes wonder *when* they will die, Suguro realized. But they never give much thought to *where* they will breathe their last.

No matter who dies in a hospital, the staff handle death as if they were mailing a package at the post office.

One evening the man in the next room, who suffered from intestinal cancer, died. For a time Suguro could hear the weeping voices of the man's family. Eventually some nurses went into the room, loaded the corpse onto a cart, and wheeled it down to the morgue. The following morning the cleaning woman was humming a tune as she sterilized the vacated room. Later that same afternoon, another patient would be admitted. No one would tell him that a man had died in his room the previous evening, and the new patient would of course have no way of obtaining that information.

The sky is cloudless. Dinner is brought around to the hospital rooms as usual, as though nothing at all has happened. On the streets below, beyond the windows of the hospital, cars and buses race by. Everyone is concealing something.

Two weeks before the day scheduled for his third operation, Suguro had his wife buy a myna bird. That particular kind of bird was considerably more expensive than a finch or a canary, and when he made the suggestion, a faint look

53

of distress flashed across her face. But she nodded 'All right,' and forced a smile. Her cheeks had become thinner over the long months of caring for her husband.

In the course of his illness, Suguro had seen this smile many times. On the day the doctor had held the still-damp X-rays up to the light and declared, 'With lesions like this, we're going to have to operate,' his wife had produced that unwavering smile in an attempt to salve his troubled mind. He had in fact been left speechless for some time when the doctors announced that they would be removing six of his ribs. In the middle of the night after that painful operation, when he had awakened still drowsy from the anaesthetic, the first thing he had seen was this smile on his wife's face. Even when the second operation ended in failure and Suguro felt completely drained of life, that smile never fled from her face.

His three years in the hospital had whittled down their bank account to virtually nothing. Undoubtedly it was inconsiderate of him to ask her to use part of their dwindling funds to buy an expensive myna bird. But right now Suguro had a reason for wanting the bird.

His wife seemed to regard the request as merely the whim of an ailing man, for she nodded and said, 'I'll get one at the department store tomorrow.'

At dusk the next day, she came into the room carrying a large package in either arm. Their son followed along behind. It was a depressingly overcast December day. One of the packages contained his freshly laundered pyjamas and underwear. He could hear the faint rustling of a bird inside the other package, which was wrapped in a cloth with an arabesque pattern.

'Was it expensive?'

'Don't worry about it. They knocked something off the price for me.'

Their five-year-old son crouched excitedly in front of the cage and peered inside.

Vivid yellow stripes trimmed the neck of the stark-black myna bird. It sat frozen on its perch, its chest feathers quivering – perhaps the train journey had been unsettling.

'Now you won't be all alone when we go home.'

Nights in the hospital were dark and long. Relatives were not allowed to stay in the rooms after 6 p.m. He always ate dinner alone, then stretched out alone on his bed, with nothing to do but stare at the ceiling.

'Feeding it is quite a business. The man told me you have to dissolve the feed in water and then shape it into a ball about the size of your thumb.'

'Won't it choke on something that big?'

'No. He said it helps them learn to imitate all kinds of voices.' She went into the kitchen provided for patients' use. Preparing part of his diet was one of her responsibilities.

The boy poked at the bird with his finger, and it crouched panic-stricken in one corner of the cage. 'Daddy, they said this bird can talk. Will you teach him to say some things before I come next time?'

Suguro smiled and nodded to his son, who had been born in the maternity ward of this hospital nearly six years before. 'Sure. What should I teach him? Would you like me to get him to say your name?'

Evening haze began to coil around the hospital room. Outside the window dim lights flickered in each of the wings of the hospital. A squeaky food wagon passed down the corridor.

Suguro's wife returned with a plate of food. 'The house is empty tonight, so we ought to be heading back.' She wrapped the plate in cellophane and set it on a chair. 'You've got to eat all of this whether you're hungry or not. You must build up your strength before the operation.'

At his mother's prodding, the boy said, 'Goodbye, Daddy. Take care of yourself.' At the door his wife turned back once more and said, 'Keep fighting.'

And that smile lit up her face again.

His room was suddenly quiet. With a flutter the myna bird darted about its cage. Sitting on his bed, Suguro peered into the mournful eyes of the bird. He recognized that it had been capricious of him, but he had several reasons for imploring his wife to buy this expensive bird.

Ever since the failure of his second operation, followed by the decision that one entire lung would have to be removed, the necessity of seeing people had pained Suguro. The doctors always spoke confidently when they talked to him about the approaching surgery, but he could tell from their expressions and from the way they avoided his eyes that the chances of success were slim. His problems were complicated by the fact that after his second abortive operation, the pleurae had adhered tightly to the walls of his chest. The greatest danger posed by the imminent surgery was the massive haemorrhaging that would occur when those adhesions were stripped away. He had already heard stories of several patients in the same predicament who had died on the operating table. He no longer had the strength to greet visitors and joke with them, feigning high spirits. A myna bird seemed the ideal companion.

As the age of forty crept up on him, Suguro began to derive pleasure from studying the eyes of dogs and birds. Viewed from one angle, those eyes seemed cold and in-human; yet from another perspective they appeared to brim with sorrow. He had once raised a pair of finches, but one of them had died. He had held the tiny bird in the palm of his hand before it expired. Once or twice it struggled to open its eyes, as though in final desperate defiance of the white membrane of death that was gradually stealing across its pupils.

He came to be aware of eyes filled with a similar sorrow observing his own life. Suguro felt particularly that those eyes had been fixed on him since the events of a day many years past. The eyes were riveted on him, as if they were trying to tell him something.

2

A bronchoscope test was one of the required pre-operative examinations. A metal tube with a mirror attached was plunged directly down the patient's throat and into the bronchi to examine them. Because of the miserable position they had to assume for the test – stretched out on the examination table with the metal rod thrust down their throats – the patients called this test 'The Barbecue'. It was all the nurses could do to hold down their victims as they writhed in pain and coughed up blood and spittle from their throats.

When the test was completed and Suguro limped back to his room, wiping the blood from his battered gums, his wife and son were waiting for him.

'Your face is as white as a sheet.'

'I had a test. The barbecued chicken thing.'

By now Suguro was numb to physical pain, and it no longer frightened him.

'Daddy, how's the myna bird?'

'He hasn't learned to say anything yet.'

Suguro sat on the edge of the bed and tried to calm his irregular breathing.

'Just before we left, Yasuko called from Ōmori. She said she and her husband were coming over today to see you.' His wife had her back to him, tying on an apron as she spoke, so he could not read the expression on her face.

'With her husband?'

'Uh-huh.'

Yasuko was his wife's cousin. Four years ago she had married an official of the Economic Planning Agency. One look at the man's sturdy neck and broad shoulders and Suguro was impressed that he had seen the model of the aggressive businessman.

Suguro lapsed into silence. His wife seemed to feel some constraint and ventured, 'Yasuko could. . . . If you're worn out from the tests, I can call and tell her not to come.'

'No, it's all right. If they're going to the trouble of coming. . . .'

He lay down on the bed. Pillowing his head on his arms, he stared up at the ceiling, which was stained with rain leaks. The borders of the stains had yellowed. It had been raining on *that* night, too. In a confessional smaller and darker than this hospital room, he had knelt down, separated by a metal grille from an old foreign priest who reeked of wine.

'*Misereatur tui Omnipotens Deus. . . .*'

The old priest lifted one hand and intoned the Latin prayer, then turned his head to the side and waited quietly for Suguro to speak.

'I . . .' Suguro began, then paused. For a long while he had debated whether to come to this chamber and confess what he had done. Finally he had summoned the courage and come here, hoping to tear off the gauze and diseased flesh that clung to his wound.

'I. . . .' *I. . . . When I was a child, I was baptized because my parents wanted me to be, not because I wanted to. As a result, I went to church for many years as a formality, because it had become a habit. But after that particular day, I knew that I could never cast off the ill-fitting clothes my parents had dressed me in.* Over the years those clothes themselves had adhered to him, and he knew that if he discarded them, he would be left with no protection for his body or his soul.

'Hurry,' the priest urged him quietly, the smells of wine and of his own foul breath spewing together from his mouth. 'The next person is waiting.'

'I haven't been to Mass for a long time. My daily actions have been lacking in charity. . . .' One after another Suguro let the inconsequential sins spill forth. 'I have not been an exemplary husband or father in my home.'

These words are absurd! I'm here on my knees muttering absolutely ridiculous phrases! Through his mind flashed the faces of friends who would mock him if they could see him now. His words were more than ridiculous – they were filled with a vile hypocrisy that had become a part of him.

This was not what he had come to say. The matter which Suguro felt compelled to confess to the one who stood beyond the reeking old priest had nothing to do with these insignificant, petty transgressions.

'Is that all?'

Suguro sensed that he was about to perform an act of even baser dishonesty.

'Yes. That's all.'

'Recite the Hail Mary three times. Do you understand? He died for the sins of us all. . . .' When he had delivered this simple admonition and prescribed the simple penance in an almost mechanical tone, the priest again lifted his hand and chanted a Latin prayer. 'Now . . . go in peace.'

Suguro got up and walked to the door of the tiny chamber. *How can they claim that a person's sins are forgiven through such a perfunctory ceremony?* He could still hear the priest saying, 'He died for the sins of us all. . . .' His knees throbbed slightly from kneeling on the floor. Behind him he sensed those sorrowful eyes, staring at him with a pain greater than he had seen in the eyes of the finch that had died in the palm of his hand. . . .

'Good morning. Good morning. Good morning!'

'You'll just confuse the poor bird if you talk that fast.' Suguro got out of bed, put on his slippers, and went out onto the veranda. He crouched next to his son in front of the birdcage. The bird had cocked its head and was listening quizzically to the boy's voice.

'Come on! "Good morning." Say "Good morning!"'

The metal birdcage reminded Suguro of the confessional. A gridwork partition just like this had separated him from the foreign priest. In the end he had not confessed what he had done. He had been unable to speak the words.

'Say it! Why won't you say it, birdie?'

'It can't say it.'

His wife looked at him, surprised by his remark. Suguro

stared at the floor. There was a knock at the door, and the white face of a woman peered in. It was Yasuko.

3

'I kept thinking we ought to come and see you. I'm really sorry. Even my husband says I'm terrible.'

Yasuko was wearing a white Ōshima kimono with a finely patterned jacket. She sat down next to her husband and balanced her handbag on her lap.

'These probably aren't any good, but try them anyway,' she said, handing Suguro's wife some cookies from Izumiya. Like Nagasakiya sponge cake, this was a confection which visitors almost invariably felt obliged to bring to a patient in hospital.

And like the cookies, the expression on the face of Yasuko's husband made it obvious that he had come solely out of a sense of obligation towards his relatives. *If I die*, Suguro thought absently, *he'll feel obliged to put on a black arm-band and come to the funeral. But the moment he gets home, he'll have Yasuko sprinkle salt on him to exorcize the pollution of death.*

'Your colour looks very good,' Yasuko was saying. 'I'm sure everything will be all right this time. Why, what could go wrong? All you have to do is convince yourself that bad luck is behind you now.' Then Yasuko turned to her husband to solicit his concurrence. 'Isn't that right?'

'Umm-hmm.'

'My husband's really the one in danger – he's never had a day's illness in his life. He's out partying late every night with business meetings and this and that. They say it's better to be sick once than never at all, so I'll bet your husband will outlive us all. You've got to be careful too, dear.'

'Ummm-hmmm.' Yasuko's husband muttered his assent as he pulled a pack of cigarettes out of his pocket. Then he glanced at Suguro and hurriedly stuffed them back.

'Go ahead and smoke. It doesn't bother me.'

'No.' He shook his head in perplexity.

Yasuko and Suguro's wife began talking amongst themselves. Their conversation apparently dealt with an old friend whom neither Suguro nor Yasuko's husband had heard of. As the topic of conversation shifted to who had married whom, and then to a recital which a certain dance teacher was giving, the two men, excluded from the discussion, could only look at one another in awkward silence.

'That's a lovely obi, Yasuko.'

'Don't be silly. It was cheap.'

Yasuko was wearing a crimson obi with her white Ōshima kimono.

'That crimson suits you very well. Where did you have it made?'

'The Mitsudaya. In Yotsuya. . . .'

This was unusual cynicism for his wife. Suguro knew that she thought it was vulgar to wear obis like this one, and he was left to wonder what had prompted this caustic remark to Yasuko. Maybe it was because she didn't have that sort of obi herself. The kimonos and obis she had brought with her when they were married had disappeared one after another. It had dawned on Suguro that without saying anything she had been selling them over the last three years while he had been in the hospital. But he realized now that simple covetousness had not been the only motivation for her remark, and he was startled.

The crimson of Yasuko's obi reminded him of the colour of blood. Blood had spattered the smock of the doctor at the little maternity clinic where he had taken Yasuko. It must have been Yasuko's blood. And, to be more precise, partly his blood, too. The blood of something that had come about between him and Yasuko.

When it had happened several years before, Suguro's wife had been in a bed in the maternity ward of this same hospital. She had not been admitted for delivery. There was considerable danger that the birth would be premature, so she had been put into the hospital for nearly two weeks. If the child were born prematurely, it would weigh less than 700 grams and would have to be cared for in an incubator, so the doctor had given his wife regular injections of special hormones.

Yasuko was still not married then, so she often came to visit Suguro's wife in the hospital. Bringing Bavarian cremes instead of Izumiya cookies. She would toss out the faded flowers in her cousin's room and replace them with roses. The studio where she studied dancing was in nearby Samon-cho, so it was no trouble for her to stop by the hospital on her way home.

Often when the bell rang to signal the end of visiting hours, Suguro would turn up the collar of his overcoat and accompany Yasuko outside. He would turn back to stare at the wing of the maternity ward. With the lights shining in each tiny window, the ward looked like a ship docking at night.

'You're going to have to go back home by yourself and eat alone, aren't you. . . ? That's miserable. You don't have a maid, do you?' Yasuko frequently commented, nestling down into her shawl.

'What am I supposed to do? I can buy a can of something and take it home.'

'If that's what you're going to do . . . I. . . . Would you like me to cook dinner for you? How about it?'

Looking back on it now, Suguro was no longer sure whether he had seduced Yasuko or she had tempted him. It made no difference. A relationship – whether love, or a union born of loneliness, or one without any special justification – had swiftly developed between them. When Suguro tugged at her arm, she had spilled over onto him, her eyes narrowed to slits, as if she had been waiting for this. They tumbled together onto the bed which had belonged to Suguro's wife before their marriage. When it was over, Yasuko had sat in front of his wife's mirror stand and, lifting her white arms to her head, had straightened her tousled hair.

The day before his wife was readmitted to the hospital for the actual delivery, Yasuko had fearfully announced to Suguro, 'I think I'm pregnant. What are we going to do?'

His face twisted disgustingly, but he said nothing.

'Oh. You're afraid, aren't you? Yes, of course you are. Because you can't tell me to go ahead and have the child.'

'That's not it . . .'

'Coward!' She began to cry.

After his wife was admitted to the hospital, Suguro returned to his deserted house and sat down alone in the small bedroom. The declining sun shone through the window and onto the two beds. One was his wife's bed, where he and Yasuko had come together in an embrace. Suddenly Suguro noticed something small and black glinting like a needle at the edge of the straw mat. It was a woman's hairpin. He had no way of knowing whether it belonged to his wife, or whether Yasuko had left it behind that day. Suguro held the small black object in the palm of his hand, staring at it for a long while.

On the advice of a friend from his middle-school days, he took Yasuko to a tiny maternity clinic in Setagaya. Unaccustomed to such matters, Suguro did not even know whether he should ask for a 'termination of pregnancy' or an 'abortion'.

'Is this your wife?' When the nurse behind the glass reception window asked the question, Suguro's face stiffened and he could not answer. Beside him, Yasuko responded clearly, 'Yes, I am.'

When she and the nurse had gone inside, he sat down in the small, chilly waiting-room. He thought about the look on Yasuko's face as she had answered, 'Yes, I am.' There had been no trace of vacillation in her expression.

A cockroach darted along the wall of the waiting-room. There was a stain like a handprint on the wall. As he flipped through the pages of the out-of-date, coverless magazine he held on his lap, Suguro's mind naturally was elsewhere.

As a baptized Catholic, he was well aware that abortion was prohibited. But he was intimidated by the possibility that his wife and family might find out what he was doing now, and learn of his relationship with Yasuko. He wanted to close his eyes to everything in order to preserve the happiness of his home. Eventually the old doctor opened the door and came out. The bloodstain that raced diagonally across his smock must have come from Yasuko. Instinctively, Suguro looked away. . . .

'We've just come back from Izu,' Yasuko was saying. 'No, not to the hot springs. I went along to carry his golf-clubs. Have you noticed I've started putting on weight? Well, he encouraged me to take up golf, since absolutely everybody is playing golf these days. But I hate doing what everyone else is doing. . . .'

Suguro's wife listened to her cousin's words with that same smile on her face. According to her husband, Yasuko had been trying since childhood to best her cousin in everything. The two girls had studied classical dance together; at a recital, Suguro's wife had danced the *Tamaya*, and Yasuko had wept because she had to dance the less showy *Sagimusume*. It therefore seemed likely that she had brought up the subject of golf now in a conscious attempt to compare her own active husband with the sickly man her cousin had married. The golf enthusiast continued to sit wordlessly across from Suguro, apparently anxious to conclude the tedious visit.

'Is this your wife?' 'Yes, I am.' On the day of Yasuko's wedding, Suguro was able to see that unruffled expression on her face once again.

The new bride and groom stood at the entrance to the hotel reception room, flanked by the go-betweens and nodding repeatedly to the guests who came to offer their congratulations. Suguro and his wife passed along the line and stood before the newlyweds. Yasuko was wearing a wedding dress of pure white. When her eyes met Suguro's, she narrowed them into slits like a Buddhist statue and peered into his face. Then she gently bowed her head.

'Con . . . gratulations,' Suguro breathed in a nearly inaudible voice. The stains on the clinic wall and the splotch of her blood on the doctor's coat darted across his mind like shadow pictures. The bridegroom stood stiff as a mannequin, his hands clasped in front of him. Suguro realized at once that this man knew nothing.

When the reception was over, Suguro and his wife walked through the deserted lobby of the hotel and went out in search of a taxi. As they passed through the door, his wife muttered as if to herself, 'What a relief for Yasuko.'

'Yes. She's got a full-time job now as a wife.' For such a mundane reply, his voice sounded a bit strained.

Then abruptly his wife said, 'Now everything will be all right . . . for you . . . and for us. . . .'

Suguro stopped and stole a quick glance back at her. For some reason that familiar smile slowly formed on his wife's face. She hurriedly climbed into the taxi that had stopped in front of them.

She knows everything. For a while the two sat side by side in the taxi without uttering a word. The smile had not melted from her lips. Suguro was unable to fathom the meaning of that smile. All he knew for sure was that his wife was not the sort of woman who would ever voice those feelings again. . . .

'Once this operation is over, everything will be all right. But you've been the real trooper, Yoshiko. . . . You've looked after him for three years now.' Yasuko turned towards the bed. 'Once you get out of the hospital, you must be especially good to your wife, or you'll be punished for it!'

'I'm already being punished,' Suguro mumbled, looking up at the ceiling. 'As you can see.'

'There, that's just what I'm talking about!' Yasuko's laugh was conspicuously loud. 'I'm always saying that to my husband, aren't I, dear? How hard all this has been on Yoshiko.'

'Not at all. I'm . . . totally insensitive to the whole thing.'

There were thorns and private meanings concealed beneath each of their remarks. But Yasuko's husband was bored, and he twiddled his thumbs on his lap. 'Don't you think we ought to be going?' he said. 'You shouldn't wear out a sick man.'

'You're right. I'm sorry. I had no idea. . . .'

Her casual remark pricked at Suguro's chest. It was a suitable end to their conversation. Yasuko's husband had 'no idea' what was going on. And the remaining three pretended to have 'no idea' what was happening, when in fact they merely refrained from saying anything out loud. They all behaved as though nothing had happened. For his sake. And for their own.

'Good morning. Good morning!' On the veranda, their son was still trying to teach the myna bird. 'Say it! Why won't you say it, birdie?'

4

Three days before the operation, the drab days were suddenly filled with activity. Nurses wheeled him off to measure the capacity and function of his lungs, and a score of blood samples were taken. They needed to know not only his blood type, but also how many minutes it would take his blood to coagulate when it began to flow from his body on the operating table.

It was early December. Since Christmas was approaching, from his room he could hear the choir from the nursing school practising carols during their lunch break. Each year on Christmas Eve the nurses sang carols for the children in the paediatrics ward.

'I suppose I should make the same preparations this time as for the other operations?' Suguro asked a young physician. An experienced surgeon would be wielding the scalpel of course, but this young doctor would be assisting.

'Well, you're an old hand at surgery now, Mr Suguro. There's really nothing you need to do to get ready.'

'They turned me into a boneless fillet of fish last time. . . .' This was how patients referred to the extraction of ribs from the chest cavity. 'This time I guess I'm going to end up a one-winged aeroplane. . . .'

The young doctor smiled wryly and turned his head towards the window. The voices of the Christmas chorus flowed in annoyingly, singing a Japanese folk-song:

> A blast of the steam whistle,
> And already my train is leaving Shimbashi . . .

'What are my odds?' Suguro spat out the question, his eyes fixed on the doctor's face. 'What are my odds of surviving this next operation?'

'This is no time to get faint-hearted. You'll be just fine.'

'Are you sure?'

'Yes. . . .' But there was a brief, painful moment of hesitation in the young doctor's voice. 'Of course I'm sure.'

> The mountains at Hakone
> Are an impregnable pass.
> Not even the impassable barrier at Han-yu
> Can compare . . .

I don't want to die. I don't want to die! No matter how painful this third operation is, I don't want to die yet. I still don't know what life means, what it is to be a human being. I'm idle and I'm lazy, and I go on deceiving myself. But, if nothing else, I have finally learned that when one person comes in contact with another, it is no simple encounter – there is always some sort of scar left behind. If I had not come in contact with my wife, or with Yasuko, their lives might have turned out very differently.

Once the doctor had gone, Suguro turned to the myna bird, which had been moved from the veranda into his room, and whispered, 'I want to live. . . !' The newspaper at the bottom of the cage was covered with white droppings and strewn with half-eaten balls of feed. The bird hunched its black body and stared at him with those sorrowful eyes. The yellowish-brown beak reminded him of the foreign priest's nose. Its face, too, resembled the face of the tippling father.

I couldn't help what happened between Yasuko and me. And I had no choice but to go to that clinic. It wasn't a sin. It was just something that happened between Yasuko and me. But as a result, one ripple has expanded into two, and two ripples have grown into three. Everyone is covering up for everyone else. . . .

The myna bird cocked its head and listened silently to his words. Just as the priest seated in the confessional had wordlessly turned his ear to listen.

But then the bird leaped to the upper perch, wagged its behind, and dropped a round turd onto the floor of the cage.

Night came. The night nurse and a doctor began looking into each room. He could hear their footsteps in the distance.

'Everything all right?'

'Yes. Just fine.'

The light from their flashlight crept along the wall of his darkened room. There was a rustle of movement as the myna bird shifted inside its covered cage.

One ripple expands into two, then three. It was he who had first cast the stone, he who had created the first ripple. And if he died during this next operation, the ripples would likely spread out further and further. The actions of a human being are never self-contained. He had built up walls of deception around everyone, and initiated lies between three individuals that could never be obliterated. It was a deceit worse than glossing over the death of someone in a hospital.

Three more days until my operation. If I survive . . . I guess I'll be spending this coming January here in the hospital, too.

In January, Suguro would turn forty.

'At forty, I no longer suffered from perplexities . . .' Confucius once wrote.

He shut his eyes and tried to force himself to sleep.

5

The morning of his operation arrived. It was still dark in his room when the nurse awakened him. He had been given a sedative the night before, and his head was heavy.

6.30 a.m. The hair is shaved off his chest in preparation for surgery. 7.30 a.m. An enema is administered. 8 a.m. An injection and three pills are given for the first stage of anaesthesia.

Suguro's wife and her mother softly opened the door to his room. They peered inside, and one of them whispered, 'I don't think he's asleep yet. . . .'

'Stupid! Do you think one shot is going to knock me out? I'm not a newcomer at this, you know.'

'You should try not to talk too much,' his mother-in-law said anxiously.

'Don't move around.'

Yasuko has probably even forgotten that I am having surgery today. With a hairclip poked in her hair like a brass fitting, she was probably heating up coffee for her public-servant husband right now.

Two young nurses came in pushing a wheeled bed. 'Well, let's go, Mr Suguro.'

'Just a minute.' He turned to his wife. 'Would you bring the birdcage in from the veranda? I suppose he's entitled to a goodbye, too.'

Everyone smiled at this jest.

'All right, all right.' His wife returned, carrying the birdcage. The bird peered out at Suguro with those penetrating eyes. *You're the only one who knows what I could not tell the old priest in the confessional. You listened to me, without even knowing what any of it meant.*

'I'm ready now.'

They lifted Suguro and laid him face-up on the bed. With a creak it started down the hallway. His wife walked alongside, pulling up the blanket that seemed ready to slide off.

'Ah, Mr Suguro. Keep smiling!' someone called after him.

They passed patients' rooms and nurses' stations on both sides, went by the kitchen, and into the elevator.

When the elevator stopped on the fifth floor, the bed gave a squeak and moved down the corridor, which reeked of disinfectant. The closed doors of the operating theatre lay just ahead.

'Well, Mrs Suguro. This is as far as you can go . . . ,' a nurse said. Family members were not allowed to proceed any further.

Suguro looked up at his wife. That smile flickered again on her drawn face. That smile, which seemed to show up on any and all occasions.

In the operating theatre his gown was stripped from him and a blindfold was placed over his eyes. When he was shifted to the hard operating table, several hands hooked down the sheet that was thrown over his body. To facilitate the insertion of needles for the intravenous blood trans-fusions, hot towels were placed on his legs to distend the vessels. Near his ears he could hear the rattle of metal instruments being arranged.

'You know how this anaesthetic works, don't you?'

'Yes.'

'All right. I'm going to place the mask over your mouth.'

A smell of rubber filled his nostrils. The rubber mask covered his nose and mouth.

'Please count after me.'

'Yes.'

'One.'

'One.'

'Two.'

'Two. . . .'

His wife's face flashed across his mind. *She knows every-thing. Is she just waiting for everything to be quietly re-solved? When did I drive her to such an extremity of self-deception . . . ?*

'. . . Five.'

'Five.'

Suguro fell into a deep sleep.

It seemed like only one or two minutes later when he opened his eyes. But it was after dark that same day before he slowly began to awaken from the anaesthetic.

Directly above him was the face of the young doctor. And his wife's smile.

'Well, hello there!' He tried to be droll, but immediately dropped back into a heavy sleep. It was nearly four in the morning when he awoke again.

'Well, hello there!' he tried a second time.

He could not see his wife. The grim-faced night nurse was wrapping the black cloth of a blood-pressure gauge around his right arm. The rubber hose of an oxygen inhaler was thrust into his nostril, and tubes from the plasma bottles trailed from his legs. There were two black holes in his left breast, vinyl tubes poking out from them. Through these tubes a noisy machine sucked the blood which was collecting in his chest cavity and siphoned it into a glass bottle. Suguro's throat was parched.

'Water . . . water, please.'

'You aren't allowed any.'

His wife tiptoed into the room with an ice-bag.

'Water, please.'

'You'll have to wait.'

'How long was I in surgery?'

'Six hours.'

He wanted to say, 'I'm sorry,' but he did not have the strength.

He felt as though enormous boulders had been stacked up on his chest. But he was accustomed to physical agony.

71

A pale streak of light illuminated the window. When he realized that dawn was near, he felt for the first time that he would survive. His luck had indeed been extraordinarily good. His joy was great.

However, he continued to spit up phlegm laced with blood. Normally, this blood would clear up within two or three days after surgery, evidence that the blood from the wound on the lung had thoroughly coagulated. But in Suguro's case, even after four or five days the thread of blood did not disappear from his spittle. And his fever would not subside.

Doctors filed one after another in and out of his room; out in the hallway they discussed his predicament in hushed tones. Suguro knew at once that they suspected a leak in his bronchi. If that were the case, various bacilli would cluster around the wound and complicate his condition with thoracic empyema. He would have to undergo surgery several more times. The doctors hastily commenced injections of antibiotics and began to administer ilotycin.

In the second week, the blood finally vanished from his phlegm and his fever gradually began to decline.

'I can tell you this now . . . ,' his surgeon smiled, sitting down on a chair next to Suguro's pillow. 'You just barely made it. This whole thing has been a dangerous feat of tightrope-walking.'

'During the operation, too?'

'Yes. In the middle of surgery your heart stopped for several seconds. That gave us a real scare. But your luck has held strong.'

'You must have accumulated many good deeds over the years, Mr Suguro,' laughed the young doctor, who stood off to one side.

After a month he was finally able to pull himself up, using the rope that hung over his bed. His legs had withered, and he was without seven ribs and one entire lung. He stroked his meagre body with his emaciated arms.

'Oh, say. What's happened to my myna bird?' he asked abruptly one day. During his long struggle with the disease, he had forgotten all about the bird. The nurses had agreed to look after it for him.

His wife lowered her eyes.

'It died.'

'How?'

'Well, after all, the nurses didn't have time to look after it. Neither did I. We fed it, but one really cold night we forgot to bring it back into the room. We shouldn't have left it out on the veranda all night.'

Suguro was silent for a few moments.

'I'm sorry. But I feel as though it took your place. . . . I buried it at home in the garden.'

He couldn't blame her. Certainly his wife had not had the leisure to fret over a bird.

'Where's the cage?'

'It's still out on the veranda.'

His head still swimming, he slid his feet into his slippers. Supporting himself with one hand on the wall, he made his way to the veranda, one step at a time. The dizziness eventually passed.

The sky was clear. Cars and buses raced along the road below. The wan summer sun trickled into the empty bird-cage. The bird's white droppings clung to the perches; the water trough was dry and stained brown. There was a smell to the deserted cage. It was the smell of the bird, of course, but the smell of Suguro's own life was also a part of it. The breathy odour of the words he had spoken to the creature that had once lived inside this cage.

'Everything will be all right now,' his wife said as she held onto him to support him.

He started to say, 'No, it won't.' But he caught himself and said nothing.

From the collection *Stained Glass Elegies*, translated from the Japanese by Van C. Gessel

chagall

Title page drawing from *My Life*, Marc Chagall

My Life

MARC CHAGALL

One fine day (but all days are fine), while my mother was putting the bread into the oven, I went up to her as she held the scoop and, taking her by her floury elbow, said:

'Mamma . . . I wish to be a painter.

'It's no good, I can't be a clerk or a book-keeper now. I'm sick of that. It's not for nothing that I had a feeling something was going to happen.

'Look, Mamma, am I a man like other men?

'What am I fit for?

'I wish to be a painter. Save me, Mamma. Come with me. Come on, come on! There's a place in town; if I'm admitted, and if I finish the course, I'll be a complete artist by the time I leave. I should be so happy!'

'What? A painter? You're mad. Let me put my bread in the oven; don't get in my way. My bread's there.'

'Mother, I can't go on. Come!'

'Let me alone.'

In the end, it is decided. We'll go to M. Penne's. And if he sees that I have talent, then we shall think about it. But if not. . . .

(I shall be a painter all the same, I thought to myself, but on my own.)

It's clear my fate is in M. Penne's hands, at least in the eyes of my mother, the head of the household. My father gave me five roubles, the monthly fee for the lessons, but he tossed them into the courtyard, and I had to run out for them.

I had discovered Penne from the platform of a tram that ran downhill towards Cathedral Square, when I was suddenly dazzled by a white inscription on a blue background: 'Penne's School of Painting.'

'Ah!' I thought, 'what a clever town our Witebsk is!'

I immediately decided to make the acquaintance of the master.

That sign was actually only a big blue placard of sheet metal, exactly like the ones you can see on shop fronts everywhere.

As a matter of fact, small visiting cards and small door plates were useless in our town. No-one paid any attention to them.

'Gourevitch Bakery and Confectionery.'

'Tobacco, All Brands.'

'Fruit and Groceries.'

'Warsaw Tailor.'

'Paris Fashions.'

'Penne the Painter's School of Painting and Design.'

It's all business.

But the last sign seemed to come from another world.

Its blue is like the blue of the sky.

And it sways in the sun and the rain.

After rolling up my tattered sketches, I set out, trembling and anxious, for Penne's studio, accompanied by my mother.

Even as I climbed his stairs I was intoxicated, overwhelmed by the smell of the paints and the paintings. Portraits on every side. The governor's wife. The governor of the town himself. Mr L . . . and Mrs L . . . , Baron K . . . with the Baroness, and many others. Did I know them?

A studio crammed with pictures from floor to ceiling. Stacks and rolls of paper are heaped on the floor too. Only the ceiling is clear.

On the ceiling, cobwebs and absolute freedom.

Here and there stand Greek plaster heads, arms, legs, ornaments, white objects, covered with dust.

Drawing from *My Life*, Marc Chagall

I feel instinctively that this artist's method is not mine.

I don't know what mine is. I haven't time to think about it.

The vitality of the figures surprises me.

Is it possible?

As I climb the stairs I touch noses, cheeks.

The master is not at home.

I shall say nothing of my mother's expression and her feelings on finding herself in an artist's studio for the first time.

Her eyes darted into every corner, she glanced at the canvases two or three times.

Suddenly she swings round to me, and almost imploringly, but in a firm clear voice, she says:

'Well, my son . . . You can see for yourself; you'll never be able to do this kind of thing. Let's go home.'

'Wait, Mamma!'

For my part, I have already decided that I will never do this kind of thing. Am I obliged to?

That's another question. But what? I don't know.

We wait for the master. He must decide my fate.

My God! If he's in a bad mood, he'll dismiss me with 'That's no good.'

(Everything is possible – be prepared, with or without Mamma!)

No-one in the studio. But someone is moving about in the other room. One of Penne's pupils, no doubt.

We go in. He hardly notices us.

'Good morning.'

'Good morning, if you like.'

He is sitting astride a chair, painting a study. I like that.

Mamma immediately asks him a question.

'Please tell me, Mr S . . . What's this painting business like? Any good?'

'Ah well . . . it's not like shopkeeping or selling, to me.'

Naturally, one couldn't expect a less cynical or less banal reply.

It was enough to convince my mother that she was right, and to instil a few drops of bitterness into me, stammering child.

But here is the dear master.

I would be lacking in talent if I could not describe him for you.

It does not matter that he is short. It only makes his profile more friendly.

The tails of his jacket hang in points down to his legs.

They float to the left, and to the right, up and down, and at the same time his watch-chain follows them.

His blond, pointed beard wags, expressing now melancholy, now a compliment, now a greeting.

We step forward. He bows casually. (One only bows carefully to the governor of the town and to the rich.)

'What can I do for you?'

'Well, I really don't know . . . he wants to be a painter

. . . He must be mad! Please look at his drawings . . . If he has any talent, then it would be worth taking lessons, but otherwise . . . Let's go home, my son.'

Penne did not bat an eyelid.

(You devil, I thought, give us a sign!)

He flicks mechanically through my copies of *Niwa* and mutters:

'Yes . . . he has some ability . . .'

Oh! You . . . I thought to myself in my turn.

My mother hardly understood any better, that's certain.

But for me, that was enough.

At all events, I got some five-rouble pieces from my father and took lessons for nearly two months in Penne's school in Witebsk.

What did I do there? I don't know.

A plaster model was hung up in front of me. I had to draw it at the same time as the others.

I set myself assiduously to this task.

I held the pencil up to my eyes, I measured and measured.

Never just right.

Voltaire's nose always hangs down.

Penne comes.

They sold paints in the shop next door. I had a box, and the tubes rolled about in it like children's corpses.

No money at all. For studies, I went to the far end of the town. The farther I went, the more frightened I grew.

Such was my fear of crossing the frontier and finding myself near military camps, that my colours became dingy, my painting turned sour.

Where are those studies on large canvases that hung above Mamma's bed: water-carriers, little houses, lanterns, processions on the hills?

It seems that because the canvas was coarse, they were put on the floor as carpets.

That's a fine thing!

We must wipe our feet. The floors have just been washed.

My sisters thought that pictures were painted for that very purpose, especially when they were done on large canvases.

I sighed, and almost decided to strangle myself.

In tears, I picked up my canvases and hung them once more at the door, but in the end they were taken up to the attic where, gradually covered with dust, they were peacefully buried for ever.

At Penne's, I was the only one to paint in violet. What's that?

Where does that idea come from?

It seemed so daring that from then on, I attended his school free of charge until, in the words of S . . . , it was no longer like shopkeeping or selling to me.

The outskirts of Witebsk. Penne.

The earth in which my parents sleep – all that is left of what was dearest to me.

I like Penne. I see his wavering silhouette.

He lives in my memory like my father. Often, when I think of the deserted streets of my town, he is in them, here or there.

More than once in front of his door, on the threshold of his house, I have longed to plead with him:

I don't want fame, I only want to be a silent craftsman like you; I would like to be hung like your paintings, in your street, near you, in your house. May I?

From *My Life*, translated from the French by Dorothy Williams

A Bright Green Field

ANNA KAVAN

In my travels I am always being confronted by a particular field. It seems that I simply can't escape it. Any journey, no matter where it begins, is apt to end towards evening in sight of this meadow, which is quite small, sloping, and in the vicinity of tall dark trees.

The meadow is always beautifully green; in the dusk it looks almost incandescent, almost a source of light, as though the blades of grass themselves radiated brightness. The vividness of the grass is always what strikes people first; it takes them a moment longer to notice that, as a matter of fact, the green is rather too intense to be pleasant, and to wonder why they did not see this before. The observation once made, it becomes obvious that for grass to be luminiferous is somewhat improper. It has no business to advertise itself so ostentatiously. Such effulgent lustre is unsuited to its humble place in the natural order, and shows that in this meadow the grass has risen above itself – grown arrogant, aggressive, too full of strength.

Its almost sensational, inappropriate brightness is always the same. Instead of changing with the seasons, as if to underline the insolence of the grass, the field's brilliance remains constant, though in other ways its aspect varies with the time and place. It is true that, besides being always bright green, the field is always small, always sloping, always near big dark trees. But size and colour are relative, different people mean different things when they speak of a small bright meadow or a big dark tree. The idea of a slope is flexible too, and though a persistent divergence from the horizontal is characteristic of the field, the degree of steepness fluctuates widely.

The slant may be imperceptible, so that one would swear the surface was as flat as a billiard-table. There have been times when I couldn't believe – until it was proved to me by measurements taken with a clinometer – that the ground was not perfectly level. On other occasions, in contrast with what may be called an invisible incline, the meadow appears to rise almost vertically.

I shall never forget seeing it so that thundery summer day, when, since early morning, I had been travelling across a great dusty plain. The train was oppressively hot, the landscape monotonous and without colour, and, during the afternoon, I fell into an uneasy doze, from which I woke to the pleasant surprise of seeing mountain slopes covered with pines and boulders. But, after the first moment, I found that, with the mountains shutting out the sky, the enclosed atmosphere of the deep ravine was just as oppressive as that of the flat country. Everything looked drab and dingy, the rocks a nondescript mottled tint, the pines the shiny blackish-green of some immensely old shabby black garment – their dense foliage, at its brightest the colour of verdigris, suggesting rot and decay, had the unmoving rigidity of a metal with the property of absorbing light, and seemed to extinguish any occasional sunbeam that penetrated the heavy clouds. Although the line kept twisting and turning, the scenery never changed, always composed of the same eternal pine forest and masses of rock, pervaded, as the plain had been, by an air of dull sterile monotony and vegetative indifference.

The train suddenly wound round another sharp bend, and came out into a more open place where the gorge widened, and I saw, straight ahead, between two cataracts of black trees, the sheer emerald wall that was the meadow, rising perpendicular, blazing with jewel-brightness, all the more resplendent for its dismal setting.

After the dim monochrome vistas at which I had been

looking all day, this sudden unexpected flare of brilliance
was so dazzling that I could not immediately identify the
curious dark shapes dotted about the field, still further
irradiated, as it was now, by the glow of the setting sun,
which broke through the clouds just as I reached the end of
my journey, making each blade of grass scintillate like a
green flame.

The field was still in full view when I emerged from the
station, a spectacular vivid background to the little town, of
which it appeared to be an important feature, the various
buildings having been kept low, and grouped as if to avoid
hiding it. Now that I was able to look more carefully, and
without the distorting and distracting effect of the train's
motion, I recognized the peculiar scattered shapes I had
already noticed as prone half-naked human bodies, spread-
eagled on the glistening bright green wall of grass. They
were bound to it by an arrangement of ropes and pulleys
that slowly drew them across its surface, and had semicircu-
lar implements of some sort fastened to their hands, which
they continually jerked in a spasmodic fashion, reminding
me of struggling flies caught in a spider's web. This tor-
mented jerking, and the fact that the grotesque sprawling
figures were chained to the tackle pulling them along, made
me think they must be those of malefactors, undergoing
some strange archaic form of punishment, conducted in
public up there on the burning green field. In this,
however, I was mistaken.

A passerby presently noticed my interest in the mysterious movements outlined so dramatically on the brilliant
green, and, seeing that I was a stranger, very civilly started
a conversation, informing me that I was not watching
criminals, as I had supposed, but labourers engaged in
cutting the grass, which grew excessively fast and strongly
in that particular field.

I was surprised that such a barbarous mowing process
should be employed merely to keep down the grass in a
small field, even though in a way, it formed part of the
town; and I inquired whether their obviously painful

exertions did not jeopardize the health and efficiency of the workers.

Yes, I was told, unfortunately the limbs, and even the lives, of the men up there were in danger, both from the effects of overstrain, and because the securing apparatus was not infrequently broken by the violence of their muscular contractions. It was regrettable, but no alternative method of mowing had so far been discovered, since the acute angle of the ground prohibited standing upon it, or even crawling across on all fours, as had at times been attempted. Of course, every reasonable precaution was taken; but, in any case, these labourers were expendable, coming from the lowest ranks of the unskilled population. I should not pay too much attention to the spasms and convulsions I was observing, as these were mainly just mimicry, a traditional miming of the sufferings endured by earlier generations of workers before the introduction of the present system. The work was now much less arduous than it looked, and performed under the most humane conditions that had as yet been devised. It might interest me to know that it was not at all unpopular; on the contrary, there was considerable competition for this form of employment, which entailed special privileges and prestige. In the event of a fatality, a generous grant was made to the dependants of the victim, who, in accordance with tradition, was always interred *in situ* – a custom dating from antiquity, and conferring additional prestige, which extended to the whole family of the deceased.

All this information was given in a brisk, matter-of-fact way that was reassuring. But I could not help feeling a trifle uneasy as I gazed at the meadow, compelled by a kind of grisly fascination to watch those twitching marionettes, dehumanized by the intervening distance, and by their own extraordinary contortions. It seemed to me that these became more tortured as the sun went down, as though a frantic haste inspired the wild uncoördinated swinging of the sickles, while the green of the grass brightened almost to phosphorescence against the dusk.

I wanted to ask why the field had to be mown at all – what would it matter if the grass grew long? How had the decision to cut it been made in the first place, all those years ago? But I hesitated to ask questions about a tradition so ancient and well-established; evidently taken for granted by everyone, it surely must have some sound rational basis I had overlooked – I was afraid of appearing dense, or imperceptive, or lacking in understanding – or so I thought. Anyhow, I hesitated until it was too late, and my informant, suddenly seeming to notice the fading light, excusing himself, hurried on his way, barely giving me time to thank him for his politeness.

Left alone, I continued to stand in the empty street, staring up, not quite at ease in my mind. The stranger's receding steps had just ceased to be audible when I realized that I had refrained from asking my questions, not for fear of appearing stupid, but because, in some part of me, I already seemed to know the answers. This discovery distracted me for the moment; and when, a few seconds later, my attention returned to the field, the row of jerking puppets had vanished.

Still I did not move on. An apathetic mood of vague melancholy had descended on me, as it often does at this hour of the changeover from day to night. The town all at once seemed peculiarly deserted and quiet, as though everyone were indoors, attending some meeting I knew nothing about. Above the roofs, the mountain loomed, gloomy, with pines flowing down to the hidden gorge, from several parts of which evening mist had begun to rise, obscuring my view of the slopes, but not of the meadow, still vividly green and distinct.

All at once, I found myself listening to the intense stillness, aware of some suspense in the ominous hush of impending thunder. Not a sound came from anywhere. There was no sign of life in the street, where the lights had not yet come on, in spite of the gathering shadows. Already the houses around me had lost their sharp outlines and seemed huddled together, as if nervously watching and waiting, and holding their breath. Mist and twilight had blotted out colours, all shapes were blurred and indefinite, so that the clear-cut bright green field stood out startlingly, mysteriously retaining the light of the departed day, concentrated in its small rectangle, floating over the roofs like a bright green flag.

Everywhere else, the invisible armies of night were assembling, massing against the houses, collecting in blacker blackness beneath the black trees. Everything was waiting breathlessly for the night to fall. But the advance of darkness was halted, stopped dead, at the edge of the meadow, arrested by sheer force of that ardent green. I expected the night to attack, to rush the meadow, to over-run it. But nothing happened. Only, I felt the tension of countless grass blades, poised in pure opposition to the invading dark. And now, in a first faint glimmer of understanding, I began to see how enormously powerful the grass up there must be, able to interrupt night's immemorial progress. Thinking of what I'd heard, I could imagine that grass might grow arrogant and far too strong, nourished as this had been; its horrid life battening on putrescence, bursting out in hundreds, thousands, of strong new blades for every single one cut.

I had a vision then of those teeming blades – blades innumerable, millions on millions of blades of grass – ceaselessly multiplying, with unnatural strength forcing their silent irresistible upward way through the earth, increasing a thousandfold with each passing minute. How fiercely they crowded into that one small field, grown unnaturally strong and destructive, destruction-fed. Turgid with life, the countless millions of blades were packed densely together, standing ready, like lances, like thickets, like trees, to resist invasion.

In the midst of the deep dusk that was almost darkness, the brilliance of that small green space appeared unnatural, uncanny. I had been staring at it so long that it seemed to start vibrating, pulsating, as if, even at this distance, the tremendous life-surge quickening it were actually visible.

Not only the dark was threatened by all that savage vitality; in my vision, I saw the field always alert, continually on the watch for a momentary slackening of the effort to check its growth, only awaiting that opportunity to burst all bounds. I saw the grass rear up like a great green grave, swollen by the corruption it had consumed, sweeping over all boundaries, spreading in all directions, destroying all other life, covering the whole world with a bright green pall, beneath which life would perish. That poison-green had to be fought, fought; cut back, cut down; daily, hourly, at any cost. There was no other defence against the mad proliferation of grass blades: no other alternative to grass, blood-bloated, grown viciously strong, poisonous and vindictive, a virulent plague, that would smother everything, everywhere, until grass, and grass only, covered the face of the globe.

It seems monstrous, a thing that should never have been possible, for grass to possess such power. It is against all the laws of nature that grass should threaten the life of the planet. How could a plant meant to creep, to be crushed underfoot, grow so arrogant, so destructive? At times the whole idea seems preposterous, absolutely crazy, a story for children, not to be taken seriously – I refuse to believe it. And yet . . . and yet . . . one can't be quite certain. . . . Who knows what may have happened in the remote past? Perhaps, in the ancient archives kept secret from us, some incident is recorded. . . . Or, still further back, before records even began, something may have deviated from the norm. . . . Some variation, of which nothing is known any more, could have let loose on the future this green threat.

One simply doesn't know what to believe. If it is all just a fantasy, why should I have seen, as in a vision, that grass, fed on the lives of bound victims, could become a threat to all life, death-swollen, and horribly strong? In the beginning, when the whole thing started, did the threat come before the victim, or vice versa? Or did both evolve simultaneously, out of a mutual need for one another? And how do I come into it? Why should I be implicated at all? It's nothing to do with me. There's nothing whatever that I can do. Yet this thing that should never have happened seems something I cannot escape. If not today or tomorrow, then the day after that, or the next, at the end of some journey one evening, I shall see the bright green field waiting for me again. As I always do.

Title story from the collection *A Bright Green Field*

A plate from *Rodin's Later Drawings, with Interpretations by Antoine Bourdelle*. 'Drawing passed over the white page like a spike of wheat over the wheatfield when the grain is ripe and from afar Rodin, the harvester, cuts and presents it, it is for us to make our bread' – Bourdelle

TOPOR

Stories and Drawings

Christmas Story

ROLAND TOPOR

Young Henry waited with beating heart behind the armchair in the drawing-room. It was three minutes to midnight. Soon he would be able to surprise Father Christmas and beg him for a mail coach to go with his electric train.

As the twelve strokes of midnight died away little bits of soot began to fall into the shoes that young Henry had put in the fireplace.

Then Father Christmas himself appeared, his fine red robe covered with soot. 'Oh dear,' he lisped in a falsetto voice, 'I'm all *dirty*!'

When he saw Henry he clapped his hands. 'Oh, what a *thweet* little boy! Hallo, little boy!'

'Hallo, Father Christmas.'

Little Henry didn't know what to say. This wasn't how he'd imagined Father Christmas. This man was young and he had a rather odd manner.

'Come and thit on my knee. I'll give you thome thweetieth.'

Father Christmas sat on the edge of the chimney-piece and young Henry obeyed at once. The sweets were delicious and the caresses that went with them were very, very nice. . . .

'Where are your parenth?' asked Father Christmas in an insidious voice.

'Mummy's gone skiing and Daddy's asleep in his room,' young Henry explained seriously.

'Fine! I'll go and thay hallo to your daddy. Go back to bed and be good.'

The man in red crept quietly into Henry's daddy's bedroom. Without a sound he took off his big boots and climbed into the bed.

'Who is it?' mumbled the father, half asleep.

'Father Chrithmath,' said Father Christmas.

And then he buggered him.

From the collection *Stories and Drawings*, translated from the French by Margaret Crosland

The following page of *Stories and Drawings* by Roland Topor. Inscribed 'and Wendy Owen amitiés de Topor' with a drawing by the artist

A drawing from *Stories and Drawings*, Roland Topor

The Other Wife

COLETTE

'For two? This way, Monsieur and Madame, there's still a table by the bay window, if Madame and Monsieur would like to enjoy the view.'

Alice followed the *maître d'hôtel*.

'Oh, yes, come on Marc, we'll feel we're having lunch on a boat at sea. . . .'

Her husband restrained her, passing his arm through hers.

'We'll be more comfortable there.'

'There? In the middle of all those people? I'd much prefer . . .'

'Please, Alice.'

He tightened his grip in so emphatic a way that she turned round.

'What's the matter with you?'

He said 'sh' very quietly, looking at her intently, and drew her towards the table in the middle.

'What is it, Marc?'

'I'll tell you, darling. Let me order lunch. Would you like shrimps? Or eggs in aspic?'

'Whatever *you* like, as you know.'

They smiled at each other, wasting the precious moments of an overworked, perspiring *maître d'hôtel* who stood near to them, suffering from a kind of St Vitus's dance.

'Shrimps,' ordered Marc. 'And then eggs and bacon. And cold chicken with cos lettuce salad. Cream cheese?

Spécialité de la maison? We'll settle for the *spécialité*. Two very strong coffees. Please give lunch to my chauffeur, we'll be leaving again at two o'clock. Cider? I don't trust it. . . . Dry champagne.'

He sighed as though he had been moving a wardrobe, gazed at the pale noonday sea, the nearly white sky, then at his wife, finding her pretty in her little Mercury-type hat with its long hanging veil.

'You're looking well, darling. And all this sea-blue colour gives you green eyes, just imagine! And you put on weight when you travel. . . . It's nice, up to a point, but only up to a point!'

Her rounded bosom swelled proudly as she leant over the table.

'Why did you stop me taking that place by the bay window?'

It did not occur to Marc Séguy to tell a lie.

'Because you'd have sat next to someone I know.'

'And whom I don't know?'

'My ex-wife.'

She could not find a word to say and opened her blue eyes wider.

'What of it, darling? It'll happen again. It's not important.'

Alice found her tongue again and asked the inevitable questions in their logical sequence.

'Did she see you? Did she know that you'd seen her? Point her out to me.'

'Don't turn round at once, I beg you, she must be looking at us. A lady with dark hair, without a hat, she must be staying at this hotel. . . . On her own, behind those children in red. . . .'

'Yes, I see.'

Sheltered behind broad-brimmed seaside hats, Alice was able to look at the woman who fifteen months earlier had still been her husband's wife. 'Incompatibility,' Marc told her. 'Oh, it was total incompatibility! We divorced like well-brought-up people, almost like friends, quietly and quickly. And I began to love you, and you were able to be happy with me. How lucky we are that in our happiness there haven't been any guilty parties or victims!'

The woman in white, with her smooth, lustrous hair over which the seaside light played in blue patches, was smoking a cigarette, her eyes half closed. Alice turned back to her husband, took some shrimps and butter and ate composedly.

'Why didn't you ever tell me,' she said after a moment's silence, 'that she had blue eyes too?'

'But I'd never thought about it!'

He kissed the hand that she stretched out to the bread basket and she blushed with pleasure. Dark-skinned and plump, she might have seemed slightly earthy, but the changing blue of her eyes, and her wavy golden hair, disguised her as a fragile and soulful blonde. She showed overwhelming gratitude to her husband. She was immodest without knowing it and her entire person revealed over-conspicuous signs of extreme happiness.

They ate and drank with good appetite and each thought that the other had forgotten the woman in white. However, Alice sometimes laughed too loudly and Marc was careful of his posture, putting his shoulders back and holding his head up. They waited some time for coffee, in silence. An incandescent stream, a narrow reflection of the high and invisible sun, moved slowly over the sea and shone with unbearable brilliance.

'She's still there, you know,' Alice whispered suddenly.

'Does she embarrass you? Would you like to have coffee somewhere else?'

'Not at all! It's she who ought to be embarrassed! And she doesn't look as though she's having a madly gay time, if you could see her. . . .'

'It's not necessary. I know that look of hers.'

'Oh, was she like that?'

He breathed smoke through his nostrils and wrinkled his brows.

'Was she like that? No. To be frank, she wasn't happy with me.'

'Well, my goodness!'

'You're delightfully generous, darling, madly generous. . . . You're an angel, you're. . . . You love me . . . I'm so proud, when I see that look in your eyes . . . yes, the look you have now. . . . She. . . . No doubt I didn't succeed in making her happy. That's all there is to it, I didn't succeed.'

'She's hard to please!'

Alice fanned herself irritably, and cast brief glances at the woman in white who was smoking, her head leaning against the back of the cane chair, her eyes closed with an expression of satisfied lassitude.

Marc shrugged his shoulders modestly.

'That's it,' he admitted. 'What can one do? We have to be sorry for people who are never happy. As for us, we're so happy. . . . Aren't we, darling?'

She didn't reply. She was looking with furtive attention at her husband's face, with its good colour and regular shape, at his thick hair, with its occasional thread of white silk, at his small, well-cared-for hands. She felt dubious for the first time, and asked herself: 'What more did she want, then?'

And until they left, while Marc was paying the bill, asking about the chauffeur and the route, she continued to watch, with envious curiosity, the lady in white, that discontented, hard-to-please, superior woman. . . .

From the collection *The Other Woman*, translated from the French by Margaret Crosland

Siddhartha

HERMANN HESSE

On the evening of that day they overtook the Samanas and requested their company and allegiance. They were accepted.

Siddhartha gave his clothes to a poor Brahmin on the road and only retained his loincloth and earth-coloured unstitched cloak. He only ate once a day and never cooked food. He fasted fourteen days. He fasted twenty-eight days. The flesh disappeared from his legs and cheeks. Strange dreams were reflected in his enlarged eyes. The nails grew long on his thin fingers and a dry, bristly beard appeared on his chin. His glance became icy when he encountered women; his lips curled with contempt when he passed through a town of well-dressed people. He saw businessmen trading, princes going to the hunt, mourners weeping over their dead, prostitutes offering themselves, doctors attending the sick, priests deciding the day for sowing, lovers making love, mothers soothing their children – and all were not worth a passing glance, everything lied, stank of lies; they were all illusions of sense, happiness and beauty. All were doomed to decay. The world tasted bitter. Life was pain.

Siddhartha had one single goal – to become empty, to become empty of thirst, desire, dreams, pleasure and sorrow – to let the Self die. No longer to be Self, to experience the peace of an emptied heart, to experience pure thought – that was his goal. When all the Self was conquered and dead, when all passions and desires were silent, then the last must awaken, the innermost of Being that is no longer Self – the great secret!

Silently Siddhartha stood in the fierce sun's rays, filled with pain and thirst, and stood until he no longer felt pain and thirst. Silently he stood in the rain, water dripping from his hair on to his freezing shoulders, on to his freezing hips and legs. And the ascetic stood until his shoulders and legs no longer froze, till they were silent, till they were still. Silently he crouched among the thorns. Blood dripped from his smarting skin, ulcers formed, and Siddhartha remained stiff, motionless, till no more blood flowed, till there was no more pricking, no more smarting.

Siddhartha sat upright and learned to save his breath, to manage with little breathing, to hold his breath. He learned, while breathing in, to quiet his heartbeat, learned to lessen his heartbeats, until there were few and hardly any more.

Instructed by the eldest of the Samanas, Siddhartha practised self-denial and meditation according to the Samana rules. A heron flew over the bamboo wood and Siddhartha took the heron into his soul, flew over forest and mountains, became a heron, ate fishes, suffered heron hunger, used heron language, died a heron's death. A dead jackal lay on the sandy shore and Siddhartha's soul slipped into its corpse; he became a dead jackal, lay on the shore, swelled, stank, decayed, was dismembered by hyenas, was picked at by vultures, became a skeleton, became dust, mingled with the atmosphere. And Siddhartha's soul returned, died, decayed, turned into dust, experienced the troubled course of the life cycle. He waited with new thirst like a hunter at a chasm where the life cycle ends, where there is an end to causes, where painless eternity begins. He killed his senses, he killed his memory, he slipped out of his Self in a thousand different forms. He was animal, carcase, stone, wood, water, and each time he reawakened. The sun or moon shone, he was again Self, swung into the life cycle, felt thirst, conquered thirst, felt new thirst.

Siddhartha learned a great deal from the Samanas; he learned many ways of losing Self. He travelled along the path of self-denial through pain, through voluntary suffering and conquering of pain, through hunger, thirst and fatigue. He travelled the way of self-denial through meditation, through the emptying of the mind of all images. Along these and other paths did he learn to travel. He lost his Self a thousand times and for days on end he dwelt in non-being. But although the paths took him away from Self, in the end they always led back to it. Although Siddhartha fled from the Self a thousand times, dwelt in nothing, dwelt in animal and stone, the return was inevitable; the hour was inevitable when he would again find himself, in sunshine or in moonlight, in shadow or in rain, and was again Self and Siddhartha, again felt the torment of the onerous life cycle.

At his side lived Govinda, his shadow; he travelled along the same path, made the same endeavours. They rarely conversed with each other apart from the necessities of their service and practices. Sometimes they went together through the villages in order to beg food for themselves and their teachers.

'What do you think, Govinda?' Siddhartha asked on one of these begging expeditions. 'Do you think we are any further? Have we reached our goal?'

Govinda replied: 'We have learned and we are still learning. You will become a great Samana, Siddhartha. You have learned each exercise quickly. The old Samanas have often appraised you. Some day you will be a holy man, Siddhartha.'

Siddhartha said: 'It does not appear so to me, my friend. What I have so far learned from the Samanas I could have learned more quickly and easily in every inn in a prostitute's quarter, amongst the carriers and dice players.'

Govinda said: 'Siddhartha is joking. How could you have learned meditation, holding of the breath and insensibility towards hunger and pain, with those wretches?'

And Siddhartha said softly, as if speaking to himself: 'What is meditation? What is abandonment of the body? What is fasting? What is the holding of breath? It is a flight from the Self, it is a temporary escape from the torment of Self. It is a temporary palliative against the pain and folly of life. The driver of oxen makes this same flight, takes this temporary drug when he drinks a few bowls of rice wine or coconut milk in the inn. He then no longer feels his Self, no longer feels the pain of life; he then experiences temporary escape. Falling asleep over his bowl of rice wine, he finds what Siddhartha and Govinda find when they escape from their bodies by long exercises and dwell in the non-Self.'

Govinda said: 'You speak thus, my friend, and yet you know that Siddhartha is no driver of oxen and a Samana is no drunkard. The drinker does indeed find escape, he does indeed find a short respite and rest, but he returns from the illusion and finds everything as it was before. He has not grown wiser, he has not gained knowledge, he has not climbed any higher.'

Siddhartha answered with a smile on his face: 'I do not know. I have never been a drunkard. But that I, Siddhartha, only find a short respite in my exercises and meditation, and am as remote from wisdom, from salvation, as a child in the womb, that, Govinda, I do know.'

On another occasion when Siddhartha left the wood with Govinda in order to beg for food for their brothers and teachers, Siddhartha began to speak and said: 'Well, Govinda, are we on the right road? Are we gaining knowledge? Are we approaching salvation? Or are we perhaps going in circles – we who thought to escape from the cycle?'

Govinda said: 'We have learned much, Siddhartha. There still remains much to learn. We are not going in circles, we are going upwards. The path is a spiral; we have already climbed many steps.'

Siddhartha replied: 'How old, do you think, is our oldest Samana, our worthy teacher?'

Govinda said: 'I think the eldest will be about sixty years old.'

And Siddhartha said: 'He is sixty years old and has not attained Nirvana. He will be seventy and eighty years old, and you and I, we shall grow as old as he, and do exercises and fast and meditate, but we will not attain Nirvana, neither he nor we. Govinda, I believe that amongst all the Samanas, probably not even one will attain Nirvana. We find consolations, we learn tricks with which we deceive ourselves, but the essential thing – the way – we do not find.'

'Do not utter such dreadful words, Siddhartha,' said Govinda. 'How could it be that amongst so many learned men, amongst so many Brahmins, amongst so many austere and worthy Samanas, amongst so many seekers, so many devoted to the inner life, so many holy men, none will find the right way?'

Siddhartha, however, said in a voice which contained as much grief as mockery, in a soft, somewhat sad, somewhat jesting voice: 'Soon, Govinda, your friend will leave the path of the Samanas along which he has travelled with you so long. I suffer thirst, Govinda, and on this long Samana path my thirst has not grown less. I have always thirsted for knowledge, I have always been full of questions. Year after year I have questioned the Brahmins, year after year I have questioned the holy Vedas. Perhaps, Govinda, it would have been equally good, equally clever and holy if I had questioned the rhinoceros or the chimpanzee. I have spent a long time and have not yet finished, in order to learn this, Govinda: that one can learn nothing. There is, so I believe, in the essence of everything, something that we cannot call learning. There is, my friend, only a knowledge – that is everywhere, that is Atman, that is in me and you and in every creature, and I am beginning to believe that this knowledge has no worse enemy than the man of knowledge, than learning.'

Thereupon Govinda stood still on the path, raised his hands and said: 'Siddhartha, do not distress your friend with such talk. Truly, your words trouble me. Think, what meaning would our holy prayers have, the venerableness of the Brahmins, the holiness of the Samanas, if, as you say, there is no learning? Siddhartha, what would become of everything, what would be holy on earth, what would be precious and sacred?'

Govinda murmured a verse to himself, a verse from one of the Upanishads:

> He whose reflective pure spirit sinks into Atman
> Knows bliss inexpressible through words.

Siddhartha was silent. He dwelt long on the words which Govinda had uttered.

Yes, he thought, standing with bowed head, what remains from all that seems holy to us? What remains? What is preserved? And he shook his head.

From *Siddhartha*, translated from the German by Hilda Rosner

Two designs from *Things I Remember*, Erté. Both are for theatrical
productions staged in the 1970s

Je suis le plus malade des surréalistes

ANAÏS NIN

It was Savonarola looking at me, as he looked in Florence in the Middle Ages while his followers burned erotic books and paintings on an immense pyre of religious scorn. It was the same drawn childish mouth of the monk, the deep-set eyes of the man living in the caverns of his separation from the world. Between us there was this holocaust burning, in his eyes the inquisitor's condemnation of all pleasure.

'You want to burn me, your eyes condemn me,' I said.

'You are Beatrice Cenci. Your eyes are too large for a human being.'

He was sitting in a deep chair in the corner of the room, his angular body struggling against the softness of the chair, looking for stones, stones to match the leanness and hardness of his bones, the petrified tautness of his nerves. Sweat was pouring from his brow. He did not wipe it off. He was sitting taut, with his vision burning in the pupil of his eye, and the intensity of the man who committed suicide every moment, but unwilling to die alone, and bringing all others down with him into his death. Unwilling to die alone, and with his eyes murdering and condemning those who did not want to die, insulting those who smiled, moved away from death.

There was a door at his right. He leaped away from my eyes and walked into the hothouse. I thought he was moved by his secret pain to vanish from us and I did not expect him to return. When he reappeared there was the scum of veronal on his lips, and his gestures were slower.

Under a Glass Bell

AND OTHER STORIES

Wendy and Peter
for a strong writer and
a daring publisher

Anaïs Nin

Half-title page from *Under a Glass Bell*, Anaïs Nin. Inscribed 'Wendy and Peter for a strong writer and a daring publisher Anaïs Nin' (the engraving is by Ian Hugo)

'I am starting a Theatre of Cruelty. I am against the objectivity of the theatre. The drama should not take place on a stage separated from the audience, but right in the centre of it, so near to them that they will feel it happening inside of themselves. The place will be round like an arena, the people sitting close to the actors. There will be no talking. Gestures, cries, music. I want scenes like the ancient rituals, which will transport people with ecstasy and terror. I want to enact such violence and cruelty that people will feel the blood in them. I want them to be so affected that they will participate. They will cry out and shout and feel with me, with all of us, the actors.'

This explosion, this shattering of the being into ecstasy and terror was what Pierre wanted to accomplish with his Theatre of Cruelty.

And I wanted to follow him. With all the fervour of my eyes I said to him I would follow him into all his inventions and creations.

Nobody would follow him. When he stood up and shouted about his theatre, they laughed. They laughed because each cell of the dream that Pierre projected was enormous, swollen out of the blood and the sea in his blood, the water of his body, his sweat and tears, his passion for the absolute. No one else believed in the absolute, no one else dared to explode to reach ecstasy. No one followed him. They laughed.

From the crystal cell in which his dream had placed me, his words, I could see his tiny figure wanting by tautness and intensity to dominate this world. I no longer heard the laughter. We were together inside of the sphere of his dream of the theatre and his dilated vision had encircled me, enchanted me.

We walked out together, out of the hall where the laughter had wounded him. We walked until we reached the outer walls of the city. A drunkard was asleep on the mud. A hungry dog was prowling. The dog began to dig into the earth, swiftly, nervously, until he dug a hole. Pierre watched him with a shudder of fear. I saw him break into perspiration, as if he were making the effort at the digging. The gaunt dog made a deep hole in the ground. Pierre watched him and then he cried: 'Stop him! He is making a tunnel. I will be caught inside of it and suffocate to death. Stop him! I can't breathe.'

I shouted at the dog who cowered away. But the hole was there and Pierre looked at it as if it were going to swallow him.

'People say that I am mad,' he said.

'You are not mad, Pierre, I see all you see, I feel all you feel. You are not mad.'

We turned away from the hole. We walked in the darkness. Pierre added to the long tunnel of his own thoughts which I could feel in the night, and they were thoughts of mistrust, mistrust of me. Every moment what I expected was the Savonarola who would explode in condemnation of me, for all that I had betrayed in my quest of the dream. He walked at my side like a severe confessor to whom I had confessed nothing because he would forgive nothing. But it was not Savonarola who appeared. It was Heliogabalus.

Pierre led me to the Louvre Museum where the paintings and statues were illuminated by spotlights, and stopped before the statue of Heliogabalus.

'Do you see the resemblance?' he asked me.

In the face of stone I saw the face of Pierre. I saw the face of Pierre when he retired behind life, behind the flesh word, into the mineral, everything drawn inward and petrified. I saw the face of Pierre in which nothing moved except the eyes, and the eyes moved like a terrified ocean, seeking wildly to withdraw also, but unable to, still liquid, still foaming and smoking, and this effort of the water in his body against the invasion and petrification of the stone, made the bitter sweat break out all over his body.

In the face of stone I saw the face of the Theatre of Cruelty. Without the liquid eyes still weeping in Pierre's face, I saw the grimace of cruelty deeply etched in the jaw.

The mouth was no longer a mouth but an open cavern in which took place great human sacrifices.

Pierre stood there and his eyes ceased to move in their orbit. They were equally transfixed. His voice began to unroll down the corridors of statues: 'Your senses are affected by a statue. In you the body and spirit are tremendously bound together, but it is the spirit that must win. I feel in you a world of unborn feelings and I will be the exorcist to awaken them. You yourself are not aware of all of them. You are calling to be awakened with all your female senses which in you are also spirit. Being what you are, you must understand what a painful joy I feel at having discovered you. Destiny has granted me more than I ever dreamed of demanding. And like all things brought by destiny it came in a fatal way, without hesitation, so beautiful that it terrifies me. My own spirit and life are made up of illuminations and eclipses which play constantly inside of me and therefore around me and on everything that I love. For those who love me I will always be a source of deep sorrow. You already observed that at times I have intuitions, swift divinations, and at other times I am absolutely blind. The simplest thing eludes me then, and you will need all the subtle understanding you have to accept this mixture of darkness and light.'

As I did not answer he added: 'I love your silences, they are like mine. You are the only being before whom I am not distressed by my own silences. You have a vehement silence, one feels it is charged with essences, it is a strangely alive silence, like a trap open over a well, from which one can hear the secret murmur of the earth itself.'

His eyes were blue with languor, and then would turn black with pain and rebellion. He was a knot of tangled nerves vibrating in all directions without a core of peace.

'I feel this moving silence of yours speaking to me and it makes me want to weep with joy. You inhabit a different domain than mine, you are my complement. If it is true that our imaginations love the same images, desire the same forms, physically and organically you are warmth whereas I am cold. You are supple, languorous, whereas I am un-yielding. I am calcined. I am like a mineral. What I fear most is that I may lose you during one of those periods when half of me is cut off from the other. What a divine joy it would be to possess a being like you who are so evanescent, so elusive.'

'Brother, brother,' I wanted to say, 'you are confusing the nature of our love for each other.'

'You will never follow me into destruction, into death.'

'I will follow you anywhere.'

'With you I might return from the abysms in which I have lived. I have struggled to reveal the workings of the soul behind life, its deaths. I have only transcribed abortions. I am myself an absolute abysm. I can only imagine myself as a being phosphorescent from all its encounters with dark-ness. I am the one who has felt most deeply the stutterings of the tongue in its relation to thought. I am the one who has best caught its slipperiness, the corners of the lost. I am the one who has reached states one never dares to name, states of soul of the damned. I have known these abortions of the spirit, the awareness of the failures, the knowledge of the times when the spirit falls into darkness, is lost. These have been the daily bread of my days, my constant obsessional quest for the irretrievable.'

Before the eyelids came down, the pupil of the eye swam upward and I could see only the whites. The eyelids fell on the white and I wondered where his eyes had gone. I feared that when he opened them again the sockets would be empty like those of Heliogabalus' statue.

He stood firm, like silex, nobly, proudly, a sudden lightning joy in the eyes when I said: 'I will follow you wherever you want. I love the pain in you. There are worlds deeper down, each time we sink and are destroyed, there are deeper worlds beneath which we only reach by dying.'

His gestures were slow, heavy, like a hypnotist. He did not touch me. His hands merely hovered over me, over my shoulder, heavy with a magnetic weight, despotic, like a command. I had come dressed in black, red and steel, with a steel bracelet and necklace, dressed as a warrior not to be touched by Pierre. I felt his desire oppressive, taut, obsessive. I felt his presence growing more powerful, huge, all iron and white flames.

'All the beauty I thought lost in the world is in you and around you. When I am near you I no longer feel my being contracting and shrivelling. This terrible fatigue which consumes me is lifted. This fatigue I feel when I am not with you is so enormous that it is like what God must have felt at the beginning of the world, seeing all the world uncreated, formless, and calling to be created. I feel a fatigue of the tongue seeking to utter impossible things until it twists itself into a knot and chokes me. I feel a fatigue at this mass of nerves seeking to uphold a world that is falling apart. I feel a fatigue at feeling, at the fervour of my dreams, the fever of my thought, the intensity of my hallucinations. A fatigue at the sufferings of others and my own. I feel my own blood thundering inside of me, I feel the horror of falling into abysms. But you and I would always fall together and I would not be afraid. We would fall into abysms, but you would carry your phosphorescences to the very bottom of the abysms. We could fall together and ascend together, far into space. I was always exhausted by my dreams, not because of the dreams, but because of the fear of not being able to return. I do need to return. I will find you everywhere. You alone can go wherever I go, into the same mysterious regions. You too know the language of the nerves, and the perceptions of the nerves. You will always know what I am saying even if I do not.'

I looked at his mouth whose edges were blackened with laudanum. Would I be drawn towards death, towards insanity? To be touched by Pierre meant to be poisoned by the poison which was destroying him. With his hands he was imprisoning my dreams because they were like his, he was laying heavy hands on me.

'You did not respond to my touch,' he accused me. 'You have become cold and distant. You are dangerous and I always knew it. I was deceived by your glidingness, your alertness, your vibrancy. You are the plumed serpent, snake and bird together, you look like spirit and yet I thought you were warm and soft. You glide with your body close to the earth and you wear your plume high in the air too, walking over the earth and through the air at the same time, waving this tiny blue plume in the air, in the dream.'

'Brother, brother,' I said. 'I have such a deep love for you, but do not touch me. I am not to be touched. You are the poet, you walk inside my dreams, I love the pain and the flame in you, but do not touch me.'

He was brought in a strait jacket and the doctor was smiling at the puzzled way he looked down at his crossed arms and his bound legs.

'Why are you so violent? Why are you afraid of coming here?'

'You are going to take my strength away, you had everything ready to take my strength away.'

'Why should I want to take your strength away?'

'Because of the white phoenix who is born every hundred years. The white phoenix is a friend of the good. And the man with the white tie who warned me of the danger he was of the order of the white phoenix who is born every hundred years and is a friend of the good. The white phoenix is now inside of me and the black eagles are envious, they are the friend of evil and they are against me. They come, six of them, in grey suits, and they pursue me. I see them sometimes in a coach, that is when it is a long time ago in a print I saw, of course today they come in an automobile. The President died today, or else I would not have been brought here.'

'The President did not die today,' said the doctor.

'Not he, perhaps, but then the other, the one who is like him.'

'There is one like him?'

'Yes, just as there is one who is exactly like me, who

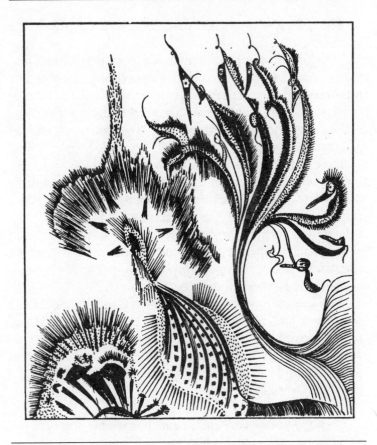

Engraving by Ian Hugo from *Under a Glass Bell* by Anaïs Nin. The artist was
Nin's husband

thinks everything I think, it is a woman, it is my betrothed,
but I can't find her.'

'Does she know you are here?'

'Not yet.'

'Who else goes after you?'

'A monk who is castrated and who sometimes takes the
form of a woman.'

'Where do you see this personage?'

'In the mirror.'

'What else do you see in the mirror?'

'The monk who is castrated and takes the form of a woman.'

'You know I don't wish you any wrong, don't you?'

'Yes, yes, I know that you have everything ready to take my strength away like Abelard.'

'Why should I want to take your strength away?'

'Because I desired my betrothed, the woman who thinks as I do.'

'How often do you see the white phoenix?'

'It is born only once in a hundred years so you see there are many more black eagles than there are white phoenixes, and so the good is always persecuted and followed by six men dressed in grey in a coach as in a print I saw, or if you prefer, in an automobile as it would be today.'

'You tried to commit suicide, didn't you?'

'Yes, because nobody loved me. I was sent to live the life of Musset and as you know he suffered a great deal and nobody loved him, and as you know he drank a great deal because nobody loved him. I was sent to live the life of Musset and to explain the prophecy he made in a café before he was hanged.'

'He was hanged?'

'Nobody knows that and I came to save his honour.'

'How can you save his honour?'

'By explaining the prophecy he made in the café before it was closed which I got from him as I stood in front of the mirror waving a white rag at the sound of the angelus.'

'The angelus?'

'I was born at noon when the angelus was ringing. White is the colour of the white phoenix and the black eagles think they are superior to him, they think they have all the power, but this power is in me now, and that is why you want to take my strength away.'

'Was that why you got violent when I wanted to bring you here?'

'No, that time it was merely to show off, because I know that you expected me to, you were expecting it so I did it, because I know all that I tell you you think it comes out of a detective story, and you know that it is true that I have read one hundred thousand novels.'

'Why did you want to die?'

'I have the blue love, because the woman who was in every way reciprocal to all that I thought did not love me, so I threw myself into the Nile in Egypt. I have many enemies.'

'Why?'

'Because when one is white like the white phoenix and the others are black one has enemies. It is always the same. It is the white phoenix that you want to take away from me.'

The doctor bade him goodbye, and told him that he could leave the room. The madman got up. The two aides stood near him. They knew that his feet were bound and that he could not walk without help, but they looked at him and made no movement towards him. They let him take two steps on his way out of the room. The doctor let him take two steps with his bound feet and smiled at the way he was tangled and bound. The madman took two steps and fell. He was permitted to fall.

From the collection *Under a Glass Bell*

A page from *The Miscreant*, Jean Cocteau (translated from the French by Dorothy Williams)

The Impostor

JEAN COCTEAU

The steep street was crowded. The Bishop, conspicuous in his cape, was already busy there. He would leave this street for nothing but his throne. He was ambitious; he enjoyed ceremony and honours. And he was not prepared to lose a scrap of his reputation.

He stood dramatically, his robe held high, showing his mauve ankles, as if the departed German flood had left puddles behind it.

He had galvanized the town, silenced the Mayor, and, captain of his vessel, he reigned supreme.

The women kissed his amethyst, the men hung on his commands. Handsome and puffed up, he was a fabulous fuchsia.

At the sight of the convoy crossing his town, he frowned, and committed to memory the appearance of the cars. The princess would have liked to receive his blessing, but Gentil was a free-thinker. He did not even believe in spiritualism, as did Madame Valiche, who was amazed at this total incredulity.

'The monster, he doesn't believe in anything,' she said.

'Oh yes,' replied the dentist witheringly, 'I do believe. I believe in vibrations in the ether.'

They thought the Bishop ridiculous.

'He's in evening dress from sunrise,' exclaimed Madame Valiche.

'Good day to you, Dominus vobiscum amen,' mumbled

the doctor, and their car passed on, the others behind it, under the hostile glare of the great man.

Towns can be burned down; bishops cannot. They paid for this mistake the following morning. At the time, the most disturbed among them was a young ordinand. He was looking for his brother, of whom he had had no news, and had been allowed to follow the convoy. He was curled up on the seat of the last car; but, as they passed, the eagle eye of the Bishop had counted every button of his cassock. He felt that he was lost. Thinking of him, Madame Valiche said to the doctor, 'Poor vobiscum, he must be at his wits' end.' She always called priests 'vobiscum'. But the doctor was asleep. Madame Valiche wrapped a shawl around him and took his lifeless hand.

The sky was pink. Cocks were crowing. Cannon shook the window-panes. Lawns, smoke, limbers, horses, were pink. Beside a field of pink beetroot, shameless dragoons were squatting down, pink moons upturned. Others in their shirt-sleeves were washing their faces. The sight of these women struck them dumb. The princess, waving her hand, stared at their pink faces, round eyes and open mouths until they were out of sight.

'We are in the wings,' she said to herself, 'and these are the actors, the walkers-on, dressing for their parts.'

They passed apple-tree after apple-tree, post after post, until they came to a straggling market-town where the casualties were being taken into a round tent pitched on the square like a circus. Madame Valiche's car stopped. She was not looking for the fire, she was looking for its victims.

The young doctors were pleased but surprised to receive this unexpected support. Someone opened a crate and handed bottles round, and the surgeon-major was informed. The surgeon-major did not look kindly on these civilians. He refused to give the princesse de Bormes the casualties she asked for.

'No, madame!' he exclaimed. 'Straw is luxury to wounded men. They need nothing else. In any case, *can't*

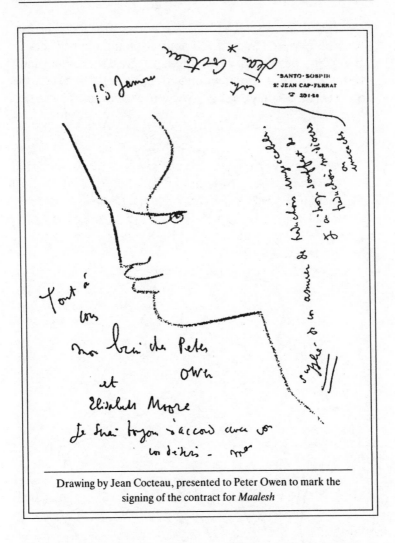

Drawing by Jean Cocteau, presented to Peter Owen to mark the
signing of the contract for *Maalesh*

the wounded be left alone? There will be a *glut* of wounded
in this war.'

All members of the convoy listened without breathing a
word. The princess was ready to burst. But it takes vulgarity to crush vulgarity. The major was insensitive to
anything else. He loathed Clémence's charm. Madame
Valiche won him over. She threw in Guillaume's name with

remarkable success. The major was transformed. His assistants unbent. The major would not hand over his casualties, but he would allow them to give the men small comforts and dress their wounds. He showed them the way to a farm nine kilometres away where the casualties were in

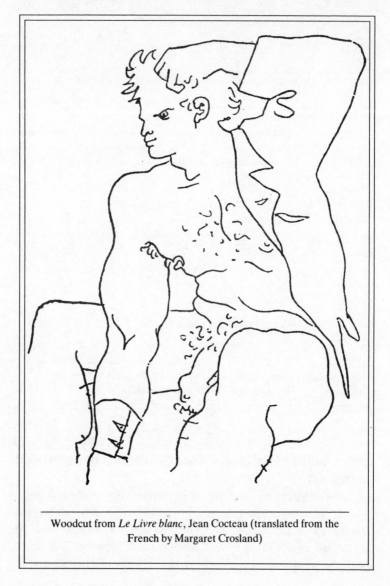

Woodcut from *Le Livre blanc*, Jean Cocteau (translated from the French by Margaret Crosland)

such bad condition that those in charge would certainly give them up.

Inside the tent about thirty martyred men lay in agony on bundles of straw. A nauseating smell prevailed, nameless, rank and sickly, tinged with the dark musk of gangrene. The faces of some were swollen, yellow, covered with flies; others had the colouring, the leanness and the gestures of El Greco's monks. They all looked as if they had just been in a fire-damp explosion. Blood was caked on their ragged uniforms, and as the uniforms had lost their precise colour and shape, it was not clear which were German soldiers and which ours. A heavy stupor made them one.

Madame de Bormes was afraid that going into such a place might make her feel sick. She made a superhuman effort to pull herself together. For she was great-granddaughter of a man who had smashed a glass and swallowed it rather than give himself up.

Madame Valiche was a real surprise. At last she was in her element. This morgue transformed her. She joked and used barrack-room language as she slit greatcoats, prepared bandages, rolled them up, brought out syringes, gave injections, and refused or gave water to the men.

'Hey, my girl!' she called to the princess, who was as awkward as Madame Valiche might have been at a ball. 'Hey, get to work! Pass me the scissors. No, no, don't unbutton that. Cut it! Cut it! The princess is paying. Not you, princess; the other.'

She laughed, kneeling by the wreck of a man.

Madame de Bormes's revulsion almost drove her to regret her undertaking. But she saw that what Madame Valiche said carried weight, that the young officers treated her as a colleague, and that she, the princess, was the one who was making a bad impression.

She looked for Guillaume. Guillaume lost no sleep over Christian charity. Armed with his name, he was inspecting the armoury and requisitioning revolvers.

From *The Impostor*, translated from the French by Dorothy Williams

Qveſt'è pur un bel cazzo, e lungho e groſſo
Deh(ſe m'hai cara laſciame'l uedère
Vegliam prouar ſe potete tenere
Queſto cezzo in la potta, e me adoſſo,
Come s'io vo prouar? ceme s'io poſſo?
Piu tòſio queſto, che mangiar ò bere
Ma s'io ui franço poi ſtando a giacere
Faroui mal? tu hai'l penſier del Roſſo
Gettati pur nel letto ó ne lo ſpazzo
Sopra di me, che ſe marphorio foſſe
O un gigante n'haurò maggior ſelrzzo
Pur che mi tocchi le midolle, e l'oſſe
Con queſto ti o ſi uenerabil cazzo
Che guariſce le potte da la toſſe
                                    Ap·ite ben le coſſe
Che potran de le donne esſer uedute
Veſlite meglio ſi, ma non fottute

Full page from *I Modi: the Sixteen Pleasures. An Erotic Album of the
Italian Renaissance*, Giulio Romano *et al*. (the text was edited and
translated from the Italian by Lynne Lawner)

Plain Pleasures

JANE BOWLES

Alva Perry was a dignified and reserved woman of Scotch and Spanish descent, in her early forties. She was still handsome, although her cheeks were too thin. Her eyes particularly were of an extraordinary clarity and beauty. She lived in her uncle's house, which had been converted into apartments, or tenements, as they were still called in her section of the country. The house stood on the side of a steep, wooded hill overlooking the main highway. A long cement staircase climbed halfway up the hill and stopped some distance below the house. It had originally led to a power station, which had since been destroyed. Mrs Perry had lived alone in her tenement since the death of her husband eleven years ago; however, she found small things to do all day long and she had somehow remained as industrious in her solitude as a woman who lives in the service of her family.

John Drake, an equally reserved person, occupied the tenement below hers. He owned a truck and engaged in free-lance work for lumber companies, as well as in the collection and delivery of milk cans for a dairy.

Mr Drake and Mrs Perry had never exchanged more than the simplest greeting in all the years that they had lived here in the hillside house.

One night Mr Drake, who was standing in the hall, heard Mrs Perry's heavy footsteps, which he had unconsciously learned to recognize. He looked up and saw her coming downstairs. She was dressed in a brown overcoat that had belonged to her dead husband, and she was hugging a paper bag to her bosom. Mr Drake offered to help her with the bag and she faltered, undecided, on the landing.

'They are only potatoes,' she said to him, 'but thank you very much. I am going to bake them out in the back yard. I have been meaning to for a long time.'

Mr Drake took the potatoes and walked with a stiff-jointed gait through the back door and down the hill to a short stretch of level land in back of the house which served as a yard. Here he put the paper bag on the ground. There was a big new incinerator smoking near the back stoop and in the center of the yard Mrs Perry's uncle had built a roofed-in pigpen faced in vivid artificial brick. Mrs Perry followed.

She thanked Mr Drake and began to gather twigs, scuttling rapidly between the edge of the woods and the pigpen, near which she was laying her fire. Mr Drake, without any further conversation, helped her to gather the twigs, so that when the fire was laid, she quite naturally invited him to wait and share the potatoes with her. He accepted and they sat in front of the fire on an overturned box.

Mr Drake kept his face averted from the fire and turned in the direction of the woods, hoping in this way to conceal somewhat his flaming-red cheeks from Mrs Perry. He was a very shy person and though his skin was naturally red all the time it turned to such deep crimson when he was in the presence of a strange woman that the change was distinctly noticeable. Mrs Perry wondered why he kept looking behind him, but she did not feel she knew him well enough to question him. She waited in vain for him to speak and then, realizing that he was not going to, she searched her own mind for something to say.

'Do you like plain ordinary pleasures?' she finally asked him gravely.

Mr Drake felt very much relieved that she had spoken and his color subsided. 'You had better first give me a clearer notion of what you mean by ordinary pleasures, and then I'll tell you how I feel about them,' he answered soberly, halting after every few words, for he was as conscientious as he was shy.

Mrs Perry hesitated. 'Plain pleasures,' she began, 'like the ones that come without crowds or fancy food.' She searched her brain for more examples. 'Plain pleasures like this potato bake instead of dancing and whiskey and bands. . . . Like a picnic but not the kind with a thousand extra things that get thrown out in a ditch because they don't get eaten up. I've seen grown people throw cakes away because they were too lazy to wrap them up and take them back home. Have you seen that go on?'

'No, I don't think so,' said Mr Drake.

'They waste a lot,' she remarked.

'Well, I do like plain pleasures,' put in Mr Drake, anxious that she should not lose the thread of the conversation.

'Don't you think that plain pleasures are closer to the heart of God?' she asked him.

He was a little embarrassed at her mentioning anything so solemn and so intimate on such short acquaintance, and he could not bring himself to answer her. Mrs Perry, who was ordinarily shut-mouthed, felt a stream of words swelling in her throat.

'My sister, Dorothy Alvarez,' she began without further introduction, 'goes to all gala affairs downtown. She has invited me to go and raise the dickens with her, but I won't go. She's the merriest one in her group and separated from her husband. They take her all the places with them. She can eat dinner in a restaurant every night if she wants to. She's crazy about fried fish and all kinds of things. I don't pay much mind to what I eat unless it's a potato bake like this. We each have only one single life which is our real life, starting at the cradle and ending at the grave. I warn Dorothy every time I see her that if she doesn't watch out her life is going to be left aching and starving on the side of the road and she's going to get to her grave without it. The farther a man follows the rainbow, the harder it is for him to get back to the life which he left starving like an old dog. Sometimes when a man gets older he has a revelation and wants awfully bad to get back to the place where he left his life, but he can't get to that place – not often. It's always better to stay alongside of your life. I told Dorothy that life was not a tree with a million different blossoms on it.' She reflected upon this for a moment in silence and then continued. 'She has a box that she puts pennies and nickels in when she thinks she's running around too much and she uses the money in the box to buy candles with for church. But that's all she'll do for her spirit, which is not enough for a grown woman.'

Mr Drake's face was strained because he was trying terribly hard to follow closely what she was saying, but he was so fearful lest she reveal some intimate secret of her sister's and later regret it that his mind was almost completely closed to everything else. He was fully prepared to stop her if she went too far.

The potatoes were done and Mrs Perry offered him two of them.

'Have some potatoes?' she said to him. The wind was colder now than when they had first sat down, and it blew around the pigpen.

'How do you feel about these cold howling nights that we have? Do you mind them?' Mrs Perry asked.

'I surely do,' said John Drake.

She looked intently at his face. 'He is as red as a cherry,' she said to herself.

'I might have preferred to live in a warm climate maybe,' Mr Drake was saying very slowly with a dreamy look in his eye, 'if I happened to believe in a lot of unnecessary changing around. A lot of going forth and back, I mean.' He blushed because he was approaching a subject that was close to his heart.

'Yes, yes, yes,' said Mrs Perry. 'A lot of switching around is no good.'

'When I was a younger man I had a chance to go way down south to Florida,' he continued. 'I had an offer to join forces with an alligator-farm project, but there was no security in the alligators. It might not have been a successful farm; it was not the risk that I minded so much, because I have always yearned to see palm trees and coconuts and the like. But I also believed that a man has to have a pretty good reason for moving around. I think that is what finally stopped me from going down to Florida and raising alligators. It was not the money, because I was not raised to give money first place. It was just that I felt then the way I do now, that if a man leaves home he must leave for some very good reason – like the boys who went to construct the Panama Canal or for any other decent reason. Otherwise I think he ought to stay in his own home town, so that nobody can say about him, "What does he think he can do here that we can't?" At least that is what I think people in a strange town would say about a man like myself if I landed there with some doubtful venture as my only excuse for leaving home. My brother don't feel that way. He never stays in one place more than three months.' He ate his potato with a woeful look in his eye, shaking his head from side to side.

Mrs Perry's mind was wandering, so that she was very much startled when he suddenly stood up and extended his hand to her.

'I'll leave now,' he said, 'but in return for the potatoes, will you come and have supper with me at a restaurant tomorrow night?'

She had not received an invitation of this kind in many years, having deliberately withdrawn from life in town, and she did not know how to answer him. 'Do you think I should do that?' she asked.

Mr Drake assured her that she should do it and she accepted his invitation. On the following afternoon, Mrs Perry waited for the bus at the foot of the short cement bridge below the house. She needed help and advice from her sister about a lavender dress which no longer fitted her. She herself had never been able to sew well and she knew little about altering women's garments. She intended to wear her dress to the restaurant where she was to meet John Drake, and she was carrying it tucked under her arm.

Dorothy Alvarez lived on a side street in one half of a two-family house. She was seated in her parlor entertaining a man when Mrs Perry rang the bell. The parlor was immaculate but difficult to rest in because of the many bright and complicated patterns of the window curtains and the furniture covers, not the least disquieting of which was an enormous orange and black flowerpot design repeated a dozen times on the linoleum floor covering.

Dorothy pulled the curtain aside and peeked out to see who was ringing her bell. She was a curly headed little person, with thick, unequal cheeks that were painted bright pink.

She was very much startled when she looked out and saw her sister, as she had not been expecting to see her until the following week.

'Oh!' Dorothy exclaimed.

'Who is it?' her guest asked.

'It's my sister. You better get out of here, because she must have something serious to talk to me about. You better go out the back door. She don't like bumping up against strangers.'

The man was vexed, and left without bidding Dorothy good-bye. She ran to the door and let Mrs Perry in.

'Sit down,' she said, pulling her into the parlor. 'Sit down and tell me what's new.' She poured some hard candy from a paper bag into a glass dish.

'I wish you would alter this dress for me or help me do it,' said Mrs Perry. 'I want it for tonight. I'm meeting Mr Drake, my neighbor, at the restaurant down the street, so I thought I could dress in your house and leave from here. If you did the alteration yourself, I'd pay you for it.'

Dorothy's face fell. 'Why do you offer to pay me for it when I'm your sister?'

Mrs Perry looked at her in silence. She did not answer, because she did not know why herself. Dorothy tried the dress on her sister and pinned it here and there. 'I'm glad you're going out at last,' she said. 'Don't you want some beads?'

'I'll take some beads if you've got a spare string.'

'Well I hope this is the right guy for you,' said Dorothy, with her customary lack of tact. 'I would give anything for you to be in love, so you would quit living in that ugly house and come and live on some street nearby. Think how different everything would be for me. You'd be jollier too if you had a husband who was dear to you. Not like the last one. . . . I suppose I'll never stop dreaming and hoping,' she added nervously because she realized, but, as always, a little too late, that her sister hated to discuss such matters. 'Don't think,' she began weakly, 'that I'm so happy here all the time. I'm not so serious and solemn as you, of course. . . .'

'I don't know what you've been talking about,' said Alva Perry, twisting impatiently. 'I'm going out to have a dinner.'

'I wish you were closer to me,' whined Dorothy. 'I get blue in this parlor some nights.'

'I don't think you get very blue,' Mrs Perry remarked briefly.

'Well, as long as you're going out, why don't you pep up?'

'I am pepped up,' replied Mrs Perry.

Mrs Perry closed the restaurant door behind her and walked the full length of the room, peering into each booth in search of her escort. He had apparently not yet arrived, so she chose an empty booth and seated herself inside on the wooden bench. After fifteen minutes she decided that he was not coming and, repressing the deep hurt that this caused her, she focused her full attention on the menu and succeeded in shutting Mr Drake from her mind. While she was reading the menu, she unhooked her string of beads and tucked them away in her purse. She had called the

A full-page wood-engraving by Michael McCurdy from *The Man Who Planted Trees*, Jean Giono. This modest paperback became a surprise bestseller when it was first published by Peter Owen in 1988

waitress and was ordering pork when Mr Drake arrived. He greeted her with a timid smile.

'I see that you are ordering your dinner,' he said, squeezing into his side of the booth. He looked with admiration at her lavender dress, which exposed her pale chest. He would have preferred that she be bareheaded because he loved women's hair. She had on an ungainly black felt hat which she always wore in every kind of weather. Mr Drake remembered with intense pleasure the potato bake in front of the fire and he was much more excited than he had imagined he would be to see her once again.

Unfortunately she did not seem to have any impulse to communicate with him and his own tongue was silenced in a very short time. They ate the first half of their meal without saying anything at all to each other. Mr Drake had ordered a bottle of sweet wine and after Mrs Perry had finished her second glass she finally spoke. 'I think they cheat you in restaurants.'

He was pleased she had made any remark at all, even though it was of an ungracious nature.

'Well, it is usually to be among the crowd that we pay large prices for small portions,' he said, much to his own surprise, for he had always considered himself a lone wolf, and his behavior had never belied this. He sensed this same quality in Mrs Perry, but he was moved by a strange desire to mingle with her among the flock.

'Well, don't you think what I say is true?' he asked hesitantly. There appeared on his face a curious, dislocated smile and he held his head in an outlandishly erect position which betrayed his state of tension.

Mrs Perry wiped her plate clean with a piece of bread. Since she was not in the habit of drinking more than once every few years, the wine was going very quickly to her head.

'What time does the bus go by the door here?' she asked in a voice that was getting remarkably loud.

'I can find out for you if you really want to know. Is there any reason why you want to know now?'

'I've got to get home some time so I can get up tomorrow morning.'

'Well, naturally I will take you home in my truck when you want to go, but I hope you won't go yet.' He leaned forward and studied her face anxiously.

'I can get home all right,' she answered him glumly, 'and it's just as good now as later.'

'Well, no, it isn't,' he said, deeply touched, because there was no longer any mistaking her distinctly inimical attitude. He felt that he must at any cost keep her with him and enlist her sympathies. The wine was contributing to this sudden aggressiveness, for it was not usually in his nature to make any effort to try to get what he wanted. He now began speaking to her earnestly and quickly.

'I want to share a full evening's entertainment with you, or even a week of entertainment,' he said, twisting nervously on his bench. 'I know where all the roadside restaurants and dance houses are situated all through the county. I am master of my truck, and no one can stop me from taking a vacation if I want to. It's a long time since I took a vacation – not since I was handed out my yearly summer vacation when I went to school. I never spent any real time in any of these roadside houses, but I know the proprietors, nearly all of them, because I have lived here all of my life. There is one dance hall that is built on a lake. I know the proprietor. If we went there, we could stray off and walk around the water, if that was agreeable to you.' His face was a brighter red than ever and he appeared to be temporarily stripped of the reserved and cautious demeanor that had so characterized him the evening before. Some quality in Mrs Perry's nature which he had only dimly perceived at first now sounded like a deep bell within himself because of her anger and he was flung backward into a forgotten and weaker state of being. His yearning for a word of kindness from her increased every minute.

Mrs Perry sat drinking her wine more and more quickly and her resentment mounted with each new glass.

'I know all the proprietors of dance houses in the county

also,' she said. 'My sister Dorothy Alvarez has them up to her house for beer when they take a holiday. I've got no need to meet anybody new or see any new places. I even know this place we are eating in from a long time ago. I had dinner here with my husband a few times.' She looked around her. 'I remember *him*,' she said, pointing a long arm at the proprietor, who had just stepped out of the kitchen.

'How are you after these many years?' she called to him.

Mr Drake was hesitant about what to do. He had not realized that Mrs Perry was getting as drunk as she seemed to be now. Ordinarily he would have felt embarrassed and would have hastened to lead her out of the restaurant, but he thought that she might be more approachable drunk and nothing else mattered to him. 'I'll stay with you for as long as you like,' he said.

His words spun around in Mrs Perry's mind. 'What are you making a bid for, anyway?' she asked him, leaning back heavily against the bench.

'Nothing dishonorable,' he said. 'On the contrary, something extremely honorable if you will accept.' Mr Drake was so distraught that he did not know exactly what he was saying, but Mrs Perry took his words to mean a proposal of marriage, which was unconsciously what he had hoped she would do. Mrs Perry looked at even this exciting offer through the smoke of her resentment.

'I suppose,' she said, smiling joylessly, 'that you would like a lady to mash your potatoes for you three times a day. But I am not a mashed-potato masher and I never have been. I would prefer,' she added, raising her voice, 'I would prefer to have *him* mash my potatoes for *me* in a big restaurant kitchen.' She nodded in the direction of the proprietor, who had remained standing in front of the kitchen door so that he could watch Mrs Perry. This time he grinned and winked his eye.

Mrs Perry fumbled through the contents of her purse in search of a handkerchief and, coming upon her sister's string of beads, she pulled them out and laid them in her gravy. 'I am not a mashed-potato masher,' she repeated, and then without warning she clambered out of the booth and lumbered down the aisle. She disappeared up a dark brown staircase at the back of the restaurant. Both Mr Drake and the proprietor assumed that she was going to the ladies' toilet.

Actually Mrs Perry was not specifically in search of the toilet, but rather for any place where she could be alone. She walked down the hall upstairs and jerked open a door on her left, closing it behind her. She stood in total darkness for a minute, and then, feeling a chain brush her forehead, she yanked at it brutally, lighting the room from a naked ceiling bulb, which she almost pulled down together with its fixtures.

She was standing at the foot of a double bed with a high Victorian headboard. She looked around her and, noticing a chair placed underneath a small window, she walked over to it and pushed the window open, securing it with a short stick; then she sat down.

'This is perfection,' she said aloud, glaring at the ugly little room. 'This is surely a gift from the Lord.' She squeezed her hands together until her knuckles were white. 'Oh, how I love it here! How I love it! How I love it!'

She flung one arm out over the window sill in a gesture of abandon, but she had not noticed that the rain was teeming down, and it soaked her lavender sleeve in a very short time.

'Mercy me!' she remarked, grinning. 'It's raining here. The people at the dinner tables don't get the rain, but I do and I like it!' She smiled benignly at the rain. She sat there half awake and half asleep and then slowly she felt a growing certainty that she could reach her own room from where she was sitting without ever returning to the restaurant. 'I have kept the pathway open all my life,' she muttered in a thick voice, 'so that I could get back.'

A few moments later she said, 'I am sitting there.' An expression of malevolent triumph transformed her face and she made a slight effort to stiffen her back. She remained for a long while in the stronghold of this fantasy, but it gradually faded and in the end dissolved. When she drew her cold shaking arm in out of the rain, the tears were streaming down her cheeks. Without ceasing to cry she crept on to the big double bed and fell asleep, face downward, with her hat on.

Meanwhile the proprietor had come quietly upstairs, hoping that he would bump into her as she came out of the ladies' toilet. He had been flattered by her attention and he judged that in her present drunken state it would be easy to sneak a kiss from her and perhaps even more. When he saw the beam of light shining under his own bedroom door, he stuck his tongue out over his lower lip and smiled. Then he tiptoed down the stairs, plotting on the way what he would tell Mr Drake.

Everyone had left the restaurant, and Mr Drake was walking up and down the aisle when the proprietor reached the bottom of the staircase.

'I am worried about my lady friend,' Mr Drake said, hurrying up to him. 'I am afraid that she may have passed out in the toilet.'

'The truth is,' the proprietor answered, 'that she has passed out in an empty bedroom upstairs. Don't worry about it. My daughter will take care of her if she wakes up feeling sick. I used to know her husband. You can't do nothing about her now.' He put his hands into his pockets and looked solemnly into Mr Drake's eyes.

Mr Drake, not being equal to such a delicate situation, paid his bill and left. Outside he crawled into his freshly painted red truck and sat listening desolately to the rain.

The next morning Mrs Perry awakened a little after sunrise. Thanks to her excellent constitution she did not feel very sick, but she lay motionless on the bed looking around her at the walls for a long time. Slowly she remembered that this room she was lying in was above the restaurant, but she did not know how she had gotten there. She remembered the dinner with Mr Drake, but not much of what she had said to him. It did not occur to her to blame him for her present circumstance. She was not hysterical at finding herself in a strange bed because, although she was a very tense and nervous woman, she possessed great depth of emotion and only certain things concerned her personally.

She felt very happy and she thought of her uncle who had passed out at a convention fifteen years ago. He had walked around the town all the morning without knowing where he was. She smiled.

After resting a little while longer, she got out of bed and clothed herself. She went into the hall and found the staircase and she descended with bated breath and a fast-beating heart, because she was so eager to get back down into the restaurant.

It was flooded with sunshine and still smelled of meat and sauce. She walked a little unsteadily down the aisle between the rows of wooden booths and tables. The tables were all bare and scrubbed clean. She looked anxiously from one to the other, hoping to select the booth they had sat in, but she was unable to choose among them. The tables were all identical. In a moment this anonymity served only to heighten her tenderness.

'John Drake,' she whispered. 'My sweet John Drake.'

Title story from the collection *Plain Pleasures*

Imp. Mourlot Fres

Robert Macaire Dentiste.

Saprelotte! M. le dentiste, vous m'avez arraché deux bonnes dents et vous avez laissé les deux mauvaises..... (Rob. à part) Diable!!! (haut) sans doute! et j'arrais mes raisons..... nous sommes toujours à temps d'arracher les mauvaises.... quand aux autres, elles auraient pu pas se gâter? ce que vous faire mal?... Un sacher postiche ne vous fera jamais souffrir et c'est bien meilleur genre, on ne porte plus que ça

---

'Robert Macaire Dentiste', a plate from *Doctors & Medicine in the Works of Daumier*, Henri Mondor

The Candles of Your Eyes

JAMES PURDY

As late as two years ago a powerfully built black man used to walk up and down East Fourth Street carrying a placard in purple and crocus letters which read:

I AM A MURDERER
Why Don't They Give Me the Chair?
Signed, Soldier

Strangers to the East Village would inquire who Soldier was and who it was he had murdered.

There were always some of us from Louisiana who had time enough to tell the inquirer Soldier's story, which evolved as much around Beaut Orleans as it did the placard-carrier.

Beauty Orleans, or Beaut, who came from the same section of Louisiana as Soldier, grew more handsome the older he got, we thought, but he was always from the time he appeared in the Village a cynosure for all eyes. At seventeen Beaut looked sometimes only thirteen. His most unusual feature, though, happened to be his eyes, which someone said reminded one of flashes of heat lightning.

How Beauty lived before Soldier took him over nobody ever tried to figure out. He had no education, no training, no skills. He wore the same clothes winter and summer, and was often even on frigid December days barefoot. In summer he put on a German undershirt which he pulled down almost as far as his knees. He found most of his clothes outside the back door of a repertory theater.

After considerable coaxing and begging Beauty agreed to settle down with Soldier in a run-down half-vacant building, not far from the Bowery.

Because of Beaut's extraordinary good looks and his strange eyes, artists were always clamoring to make drawings of him.

His friend Soldier, whose own eyes were the color of slightly new pennies, protected or perhaps imprisoned Beaut out of his love for the boy. If you wanted to get permission to draw Beaut, you had to go straight to Soldier first and finagle the arrangements.

Soldier would hesitate a long while with a suing artist, would leaf through an old ledger he had found in the same theater Beaut got his clothes from, and finally, after arguing and scolding, would arrive at a just price, and Beaut was begrudgingly allowed to leave for a calculated number of hours.

I don't know which of the two loved the other the most, Beaut Soldier or Soldier Beaut.

Soldier used to hold Beaut in his arms and lullaby him in a big rocking chair which they had found in good shape left behind on the street by looters.

He rocked Beaut in the chair as one would a doll. It was their chief occupation, their sole entertainment. It was an unforgettable sight, midnight-black strapping Soldier holding the somewhat delicate, though really tough, Beaut. If you looked in on them in the dark, you seemed to see only Beaut asleep in what looked like the dark branches of a tree.

Soldier earned for them both, either by begging or stealing. But he was not considered a professional thief even by the police. Just light-fingered when the need was pressing.

Soldier insisted Beaut always wear a gold chain he had picked up from somewhere, but the younger man did not like the feel of metal against his throat. He said it reminded him of a gun pointed at him. But in the end he gave in and wore the chain.

People in the Village wondered how these two could go on so long together. But it was finally understood that Beaut and Soldier had reached some kind of perfection in their love for one another. They had no future, and no past – just the *now* in which Soldier rocked Beauty on his knees and kissed his smooth satiny reddish-gold hair.

'Beaut,' Soldier said once near the end of their time together, gazing at him out of his brown-penny eyes, 'you are my morning, noon, and night. But especially noon, you hear? Broad noon. Why, if the sun went out, and no stars shined, and I had you, Beaut, I wouldn't give a snap if all them luminaries was snuffed out. You'd shine to make me think they was still out there blazin'.'

Then he would rock Beaut and lullaby him as the night settled down over the city.

We knew it couldn't last. Nothing perfect and beautiful has any future. And these two were already overdue in their paradise together. Doom is what perfect love is always headed for.

So then one night Soldier did not come back to that shell of a building they had lived together in.

Beaut stirred after a while in the chair, like a child in his mother's body wanting to be born. Still, no Soldier.

Hunger at last drove Beaut out into the street. Outside, he rubbed his eyes and stared about as if he had been asleep for many considerable years.

'Where's Soldier?' he asked of everybody he met, friend or total stranger.

By way of reply, we gave him food and drink. No one thought to rock him.

As days and weeks passed, the young boy got older-looking, but if anything more beautiful. His eyes located deep in his skull looked like little birthday candles flickering. A few wrinkles began forming around those candlelike eyes. Some of his teeth came out, but he looked handsome still even without them.

All he ever said when he said anything was 'Where is Soldier at?'

Beaut stole some reading glasses from a secondhand store in order to go over the ledger which Soldier had left behind and into which his black friend was accustomed to put down sentences when he was not rocking Beaut.

But the sentences in the ledger, it appeared, all said the same thing over and again, often in the same wording, like the copybook of a schoolboy who is learning to spell.

The sentences read: 'Soldier loves Beaut. He's my sky and land and deep blue sea. Beaut, don't ever leave me. Beaut, never stop loving me and letting me love you. You hear me?'

Beaut rocked in the chair, singing his own lullaby to himself. He broke his glasses, but managed to read the ledger anyhow, for in any case he had got by heart the few repeated sentences Soldier had put down in it.

'He'll come back,' Beaut told Orley Austin, a Negro ex-boxer from Mississippi. 'I know Soldier.'

One day Orley came into the room with the rocking chair, and closed the door loudly behind him. He looked at Beaut. He spat on his palms and rubbed them together vigorously.

'Say,' Beaut raised his voice. Orley bent down and kissed Beaut on the crown of his head, and put his right hand over Beaut's heart, thus testifying he had come to take Soldier's place in the rocking-chair room.

So they began where Soldier had left off, the new lover and Beaut together, but though the younger man was not so lonesome with Orley around, you could see he was not quite as satisfied with the ex-boxer as he had been with Soldier – despite the fact that if anything Orley rocked Beaut more than Soldier had. He could rock him all night long because he smoked too much stuff.

Then you remember that terrible winter that broke all weather records. Usually New York doesn't have such fierce cold as say Boston or northern Maine, though for those from Louisiana even a little taste of Northern winter is too much. And you have got to remember the house with the rocking-chair room didn't have much in the way of a furnace. The pipes all froze, the front windows turned to a kind of iceberg, and even the rats were found ice-stiff on the stairs.

Ice hung from the big high ceiling like it had grown chandeliers.

The staircase collapsed from broken pipes and accumulations of giant icicles.

At the first break in the weather, wouldn't you know, Soldier returned. He had some difficulty getting to the upstairs on account of there was no stairs now, only piles of lumber, but he crawled and crept his way up to the rocking-chair room.

What he saw froze him like the ice had frozen the house.

He saw his place taken by Orley, who was holding Beaut in his arms in the chair, their lips pressed tightly together, their hands holding one another more securely than Soldier had ever dared hold Beaut. They looked to him like flowers under deep mountain streams, but motionless like the moon in November.

'Explain me' was all Soldier was able to get out from his lips. 'Explain me!'

When they did not answer, and did not so much as open their eyes, he brought out his stolen gun.

'Tell me what I am lookin' at ain't so,' he thought he said to them.

When nobody spoke, he cocked his gun.

He waited another minute in the silence, then he fired all the bullets. But as they flew through the melting air, he saw something was wrong even with the bullets, for though they hit their target, their target deflected them like stone, not flesh and blood.

We have decided that Soldier had gone crazy even before he emptied the gun on the two lovers, but the realization his bullets did not reach flesh and blood caused him to lose his mind completely.

After the shooting he went to the police station and

charged himself. The police hardly said two words to him, and took down nothing he said. But they did finally get around to going to the rocking-chair room in their own good time. They must have seen at once that Beaut and Orley had been dead for days, maybe weeks, long before Soldier reached them. No gun can kill people who have frozen to death.

Every day for many weeks Soldier went to the police precinct and confessed to murder. Some of the cops even pretended to take down what he said. They gave him cigarettes and bottled soda.

Soldier lives in a different building now with an older white boy. But every day, especially on Sundays, he carries up and down Fourth Street this placard, whose letters are beginning to fade:

I AM A MURDERER
Why Don't They Give Me the Chair?

Title story from the collection *The Candles of Your Eyes*

1919 133

OPPRESSED LITTLE GENTLEMAN, 1919, 133

Drawing from *The Diaries of Paul Klee, 1898–1918*, edited by Felix
Klee (translated from the German by Pierre Schneider *et al.*)

The Ice Palace

TARJEI VESAAS

The roar was suddenly stronger. The river began to quicken its speed, flowing in yellow channels. Unn ran down the slope alongside, in a silvered confusion of heather and grass tussocks, an occasional tree among them. The roar was stronger, thick whorls of spray rose up abruptly in front of her – she was at the top of the falls.

She stopped short as if about to fall over the edge, so abruptly did it appear.

Two waves went through her: first the paralysing cold, then the reviving warmth – as happens on great occasions.

Unn was there for the first time. No one had asked her to come here with them during the summer. Auntie had mentioned that there was a waterfall, no more. There had been no discussion of it until now, in the late autumn at school, after the ice palace had come and was worth seeing.

And what was this?

It must be the ice palace.

The sun had suddenly disappeared. There was a ravine with steep sides; the sun would perhaps reach into it later, but now it was in ice-cold shadow. Unn looked down into an enchanted world of small pinnacles, gables, frosted domes, soft curves and confused tracery. All of it was ice, and the water spurted between, building it up continually. Branches of the waterfall had been diverted and rushed into new channels, creating new forms. Everything shone. The sun had not yet come, but it shone ice-blue and green of itself, and deathly cold. The waterfall plunged into the middle of it as if diving into a black cellar. Up on the edge of the rock the water spread out in stripes, the colour changing from black to green, from green to yellow and white, as the fall became wilder. A booming came from the cellar-hole where the water dashed itself into white foam against the stones on the bottom. Huge puffs of mist rose into the air.

Unn began to shout for joy. It was drowned in the surge and din, just as her warm clouds of breath were swallowed up by the cold spume.

The spume and the spray at each side did not stop for an instant, but went on building minutely and surely, though frenziedly. The water was taken out of its course to build with the help of the frost: larger, taller, alcoves and passages and alleyways, and domes of ice above them; far more intricate and splendid than anything Unn had ever seen before.

She was looking right down on it. She had to see it from below, and she began to climb down the steep, rimed slope at the side of the waterfall. She was completely absorbed by the palace, so stupendous did it appear to her.

Only when she was down at the foot of it did she see it as a little girl on the ground would see it, and every scrap of guilty conscience vanished. She could not help thinking that nothing had been more right than to go there. The enormous ice palace proved to be seven times bigger and more extravagant from this angle.

From here the ice walls seemed to touch the sky; they grew as she thought about them. She was intoxicated. The palace was full of wings and turrets, how many it was impossible to say. The water had made it swell in all directions, and the main waterfall plunged down in the middle, keeping a space clear for itself.

There were places that the water had abandoned, so that they were completed, shining and dry. Others were covered in spume and water drops, and trickling moisture that in a flash turned into blue-green ice.

It was an enchanted palace. She must try to find a way in!

It was bound to be full of curious passages and doorways – and she must get in. It looked so extraordinary that Unn forgot everything else as she stood in front of it. She was aware of nothing but her desire to enter.

But finding the way was not so simple. Many places that looked like openings cheated her, but she did not give up, and so she found a fissure with water trickling through it, wide enough to squeeze herself through.

Unn's heart was thudding as she entered the first room.

Green, with shafts of subdued light penetrating here and there; empty but for the biting cold. There was something sinister about the room.

Without thinking she shouted 'Hey!', calling for someone. The emptiness had that effect; you had to shout in it. She did not know why, she knew there was nobody there.

The reply came at once. 'Hey!' answered the room weakly.

How she started!

One might have expected the room to be as quiet as the tomb, but it was filled with an even roaring. The noise of the waterfall penetrated the mass of ice. The wild play of the water outside, dashing itself to foam against the stones on the bottom, was a low, dangerous churning in here.

Unn stood for a little to let her fright ebb away. She did not know what she had called to and did not know what had answered her. It could not have been an ordinary echo.

Perhaps the room was not so large after all? It felt large. She did not try to see whether she could get more answers, instead she looked for a way out, a means of getting further in. It did not occur to her for a moment to squeeze out into the daylight again.

And she found a way as soon as she looked for it: a large fissure between polished columns of ice.

She emerged into a room that was more like a passage, but was a room all the same. She tested it with a half-whispered 'Hey!' and got a half-frightened 'Hey!' back again. She knew that rooms like this belonged in palaces –

she was bewitched and ensnared, and let what had been lie behind her. At this moment she thought only of palaces.

She did not shout 'Siss!' in the dark passage, she shouted 'Hey!' She did not think about Siss in this unexpected enchantment, she thought about room upon room in a green ice palace, and that she must enter each one of them.

The cold was piercing, and she tried to see whether she could make big clouds with her breath, but the light was too dim. Here the noise of the waterfall came from below – but that couldn't be right? Nothing was right in such a palace, but you seemed to accept it.

She had to admit she was a little chilled and shivering, in spite of the warm coat Auntie had given her when the wintry weather had set in this autumn. But she would soon forget about it in the excitement of the next room, and the room was to be found, as surely as she was Unn.

As might be expected in a narrow room, there was a way out at the other end: green, dry ice, a fissure abandoned by the water.

When she arrived inside the next one she caught her breath at what she saw: she was in the middle of a petrified forest. An ice forest.

The water, which had spurted up here for a while, had fashioned stems and branches of ice, and small trees stuck up from the bottom among the large ones. There were things here too that could not be described as either the one or the other – but they belonged to such a place and one had to accept everything as it came. She stared wide-eyed into a strange fairy-tale. The water was roaring far away.

The room was light. No sunshine – it was probably still behind the hill – but the daylight sidled in, glimmering curiously through the ice walls. It was dreadfully cold.

But the cold was of no importance as long as she was there; that was how it should be, this was the home of the cold. Unn looked round-eyed at the forest, and here too she gave a faltering and tentative shout: 'Hey!'

There was no reply.

She started in surprise. It didn't answer!

Everything was stone-hard ice. Everything was unusual. But it did not answer, and that was not right. She shuddered, and felt herself to be in danger.

The forest was hostile. The room was magnificent beyond belief, but it was hostile and it frightened her. She looked for a way out at once, before anything should happen. Forward or back meant nothing to her any longer; she had lost all sense of it.

And she found another fissure to squeeze through. They seemed to open up for her wherever she went. When she was through she was met by a new kind of light that she was to recognize from her past life: it was ordinary daylight.

She looked about her hastily, a little disappointed; it was the ordinary sky above her! No ceiling of ice, but a cold blue winter sky reassuringly high up. She was in a round room with smooth walls of ice. The water had been here, but had been channelled elsewhere afterwards.

Unn did not dare to shout 'Hey!' here. The ice forest had put a stop to that, but she stood and tested her clouds of breath in this ordinary light. She felt colder and colder when she remembered to think about it. The warmth from her walk had been used up long ago, the warmth inside her was now in these small clouds of breath. She let them rise up in quick succession.

She was about to go on, but stopped abruptly. Someone had called 'Hey!' From *that* direction. She spun round and found no one. But she had not imagined it.

She supposed that if the visitor did not call, then the room did so. She was not sure she liked it, but answered with a soft 'Hey!' really no more than a whisper.

But it made her feel better. She seemed to have done the right thing, so she took courage from it and looked round for a fissure so that she could go on at once. The roar of the falling water was loud and deep at this point; she was close to it without being able to see it. She must go on!

Unn was shivering with cold now, but she did not know it, she was much too excited. There was the opening! As soon as she wanted one it was there.

Through it quickly.

But this was unexpected too: she was standing in what looked like a room of tears.

As soon as she stepped in she felt a trickling drop on the back of her neck. The opening she had come through was so low that she had had to bend double.

It was a room of tears. The light in the glass walls was very weak, and the whole room seemed to trickle and weep with these falling drops in the half dark. Nothing had been built up there yet, the drops fell from the roof with a soft splash, down into each little pool of tears. It was all very sad.

They fell into her coat and her woollen cap. It didn't matter, but her heart was heavy as lead. It was weeping. What was it weeping for?

It must stop!

It did not stop. On the contrary, it seemed to increase. The water was coming in this direction in greater quantities, the trickling went faster, the tears fell copiously.

It began oozing down the walls. She felt as if her heart would break.

Unn knew well enough that it was water, but it was a room of tears just the same. It made her sadder and sadder: it was no use calling anyone or being called in a room like this. She did not even notice the roar of the water.

The drops turned to ice on her coat. In deep distress she tried to leave. She stumbled along the walls, and at once she found the way out – or the way in, for all she knew.

A way out which was narrower than any of the others through which she had squeezed, but which looked as if it led into a brightly lit hall. Unn could just see it, and she was wild with the desire to enter it; it seemed to be a matter of life and death.

Too narrow, she could not get through. But she had to get in. It's the thick coat, she thought, and tore off the coat and satchel, leaving them to lie there until she came back. She did not think much about that, in any case, only about getting in.

And now she managed it, slender and supple as she was, when she pushed hard enough.

The new room was a miracle, it seemed to her. The light shone strong and green through the walls and the ceiling, raising her spirits after their drenching in the tears.

Of course! Suddenly she understood, now she could see it clearly: it had been herself crying so hard in there. She did not know why, but it had been herself, plunged in her own tears.

It was nothing to bother about. It had just been a pause in the doorway as she stepped into this clean-swept room, luminous with green light. Not a drop on the ceiling here, and the roar of the waterfall was muffled. This room seemed to be made for shouting in, if you had something to shout about, a wild shout about companionship and comfort.

It gushed out, she called 'Siss!'

When she had done so she started. 'Siss!' came in answer from at least three directions.

She stood still until the shout mingled with the roar. Then she crossed the room. As she did so she thought about her mother, and about Siss, and about the other – she managed it for a very brief moment. The call had made an opening; now it slammed shut again.

Why am I here? It occurred to her, as she walked up and down. Not so many steps, she was walking more and more stiffly and unrecognizably. Why am I here? She attempted to find the solution to this riddle. Meanwhile she walked, strangely exalted, half unconscious.

She was close to the edge now: the ice laid its hand upon her.

She sensed the paralysing frost. Her coat had been left somewhere else, that was the reason. Now the cold could bore into her body as it liked. She felt herself getting frightened, and darted across to the wall to get out to her warm coat. Where had she come in?

The wall was a mountain of ice, compact and smooth. She darted across to another. How many walls were there? All was compact and smooth wherever she turned. She began shouting childishly, 'I must get out!' Immediately she found the opening.

But this palace was odd: she did not get back to her coat, she came out into something she did not like very much.

Yet another room. It was really tiny, and full of dripping icicles hanging down from the low ceiling, full of icicles growing up from the floor, and jagged walls with many angles, so thick that the green light was deadened. But the roar of the waterfall was not deadened, here it was suddenly very close, or underneath, or wherever it might be – it was like being right *inside* it.

The water trickled down the walls of this room, reminding her of the one in which she had cried. She did not cry now. The cold prevented that and blurred everything. Much was flashing through her mind, but as if in a mist; if she tried to grasp it, something else was there instead. It must have occurred to her that surely this was dangerous, she would shout loudly and challengingly the shout that was part of the ice palace: 'Hey! Hey!'

But it could scarcely be called a proper shout. Another thought laid itself across it, and she barely heard it herself. It did not carry at all; the only answer was the savage roar. The roar swept all other sounds away. Nor did it matter. Another thought, and another ray of cold had already chopped it off.

It occurred to her that the roar was like something to lie down in, just to lie down in and be carried away. As far as you wanted to – no, that one was chopped off.

The floor was wet with the drops. In some places the surface of the water was freezing thinly. *This* was no place to be – Unn searched the complicated walls yet again for an opening.

This was the last room; she could go no further.

She thought this only vaguely. At any rate there was no way out. This time it was no use, whatever she did. There were plenty of fissures, but they did not lead out to anything, only further in to ice and strange flashes of light.

But she had come in, after all?

No use thinking like that. It was not in, it was out now – and that was another matter, she thought confusedly. The fissure through which she had entered was naturally not to be found when she wanted to leave again.

No use calling, the roar drowned it. A hollow of tears was ready waiting in front of her. She could plunge into it, but she could not drag herself so far. She had finished with that elsewhere.

Was someone knocking on the wall?

No, nobody would knock on the wall here! You don't knock on walls of ice. What she was looking for was a dry patch to stand on.

At last she found a corner where there was no moisture, but dry frost. There she sat down with her feet tucked under her, her feet, which she could no longer feel.

Now the cold began to stiffen her whole body, and she no longer felt it so keenly. She felt tired, and had to sit down for a while before she began looking seriously for the way out and an escape – away from here – out to her coat and out to Auntie and out to Siss.

Her thoughts became gradually more confused and vague. She distinguished Mother for a while, then she slid away too. And all the rest was a mist, threaded with flashes, but not so as to hold her attention. There would be time enough to think about it later.

Everything was so long ago, it receded. She was tired of all this running about in the palace, in all this strangeness, so it was good to sit for a while, now that the cold was not troubling her so much. She sat squeezing her hands together hard. She had forgotten why. After all, she was wearing her double mitts.

The drops began to play to her. At first she had heard nothing besides the tremendous roar, but now she could

distinguish the plim-plam of the falling drops. They oozed
out of the low ceiling and fell on to icicles and into puddles –
and there was a song in it, monotonous and incessant:
plim-plam, plim-plam.

And what was *that*?

She straightened up. Something was flooding over her
that she had never felt before, she began to shout – now she
had a deep, black well of shouts if she should need them –
but she did not let out more than one.

There was something in the ice! At first it had no form,
but the moment she shouted it took shape, and shone out
like an eye of ice up there, confronting her, putting a stop
to her thoughts.

It was clearly an eye, a tremendous eye.

It grew wider and wider as it looked at her, right in the
middle of the ice, and full of light. That was why she had
shouted only once. And yet when she looked again it was
not frightening.

Her thoughts were simple now. The cold had paralysed
them little by little. The eye in the ice was big and looked at
her unblinkingly, but there was no need to be afraid, all she
thought was: What are you looking for? Here I am. More
hazily a familiar thought in such situations came to her: I
haven't done anything.

No need to be afraid.

She settled down again as before, with her feet drawn up,
and looked about her, for the eye was bringing more light,
the room was more distinct.

It's only a big eye.

There *are* big eyes here.

But she felt it looking at her from up there, and she was
obliged to raise her head and meet the eye without
flinching.

Here I am. I've been here all the time. I haven't done
anything.

Gradually the room filled with the plim-plam of the water drops. Each drop was like a fraction of a song. Beneath played the harsh, incessant roar, and then came the high plim-plam, like more pleasant music in the middle of it. It reminded her of something she had forgotten a long time ago, and because of that it was familiar and reassuring.

The light increased.

The eye confronted her, giving out more light. But Unn looked at it boldly, letting it widen as much as it would, letting it inspect her as closely as it wished; she was not afraid of it.

She was not cold either. She was not comfortable, she was strangely paralysed, but she did not feel cold. Hazily she remembered a time when it had been dreadfully cold in the palace, but not now. She felt quite heavy and limp, she really would have liked to sleep for a little, but the eye kept her awake.

Now she no longer stirred, but sat against the wall with her head raised so that she could look straight at the light in the ice. The light became increasingly brighter and began to fill up with fire. Between herself and the eye were the quick glints of the falling drops as they made their monotonous music.

The fiery eye had been merely a warning, for now the room was suddenly drowned in flame. The winter sun was at last high enough to enter the ice palace.

The late, cold sun retained a surprising amount of its strength. Its rays penetrated thick ice walls and corners and fissures, and broke the light into wonderful patterns and colours, making the sad room dance. The icicles hanging from the ceiling and the ones growing up from the floor, and the water drops themselves all danced together in the flood of light that broke in. And the drops shone and hardened and shone and hardened, making one drop the less each time in the little room. It would soon be filled.

A blinding flood of light. Unn had lost all ties with everything but light. The staring eye had burned up, everything was light. She thought dully that there was an awful lot of it.

She was ready for sleep, she was even warm as well. It was not cold in here at any rate. The pattern in the ice wall danced in the room, the light shone more strongly. Everything that should have been upright was upside-down – everything was piercingly bright. Not once did she think this was strange; it was just as it should be. She wanted to sleep; she was languid and limp and ready.

From *The Ice Palace*, translated from the Norwegian by Elizabeth Rokkan

THE SOUTH SEAS
(To Augusto Monti)

One evening we walked along the side of a hill
in silence. In the late evening dusk
my cousin was a giant dressed in white
with a bronzed face, he moved quietly,
silently. Silence is our strength.
One of us was surely often alone –
some great man among half-wits or a poor lunatic –
to teach so much silence to his family.

Facsimile manuscript page of 'The South Seas' from *A Mania for Solitude:
Selected Poems 1930–1950*, Cesare Pavese. Translated from the Italian by
Margaret Crosland

Summer Storm

CESARE PAVESE

The sun had not yet reached the bathing-hut on the landing-stage at the foot of the hills. Great trees over-shadowed it. The river gleamed an even white in the dawn, and on the far bank houses in scattered suburbs began to show lights. Over there it seemed broad daylight already. The old boat-woman, dirty and dishevelled, was going along the line of punts moored to the landing-stage, pulling them in, one by one, then bending forward with her left hand on her hip to haul in the slack ropes. Every time a boat wedged itself between two others, the bump was passed along the whole line, setting them all rocking in the current.

A hessian curtain hung across the back of the hut and from behind it came sounds of movements and voices. Somebody was undressing.

'Look at this silk blouse! Is it yours?' a harsh voice cried. 'And these silk stockings?'

The old woman looked up crossly, stopping her work. The reflection from a few pink clouds above the trees shone on the river and cast a glow over her face.

'Here's a skirt, too,' the voice went on. 'Lovely quality! And another one!'

The curtain was pulled aside and a young fellow came out, buttoning the shoulder of his swimming costume. He was short and not very muscular, but sunburnt and curly haired.

'And we meant to be first, this time! Gosh! It's cold,

here,' he said, slapping his thighs, all pimply with goose-flesh, and jumping up and down. 'We talked about making it a foursome if we could get a couple of girls out of bed this early and take them boating.'

'There's a couple of girls ahead of you, all by themselves,' the old woman told him, bending to her work again. 'Alone and full of beans. Since no one was here to see them they didn't mind waking people up before it was light. They didn't even give me time to comb my hair. Women!'

'Alone!' the young fellow cried as he jumped about. 'D'you hear that, Moro? Two girls on their own ahead of us! Come on out of there!' He turned and asked the old woman: 'What are they like? What sort are they?'

'Haven't you just seen their clothes?' she answered with a grin. 'From a woman's slip to her skin is no great distance.'

'That's nothing to go by. Who are they?'

'They aren't regular customers. One is thin, her hair and skin as pale as straw. The other hadn't much to say but she's already tanned dark brown by the sun, well-built and so full of energy that she almost capsized the boat when she jumped in. Both of them were very stuck-up and stand-offish.'

'Have they been gone long?'

'An hour or so.'

'Pretty? What colour bathing costumes?'

'Ask her if they took their handbags with them, Aurelio,' the first voice called sharply from behind the curtain.

'That friend of yours sounds a bright lad,' the old woman chuckled with a wink. Raising her voice she added: 'Don't worry. They can pay for their own boat. They look as if they're worth much more than that.'

'Depends who they come across,' and the second man emerged from behind the curtain, a tall, bony fellow with great sweaty feet and red hands, fastening his baggy swim-suit over shoulders as pale as the belly of a fish. He looked straight at the old woman, whose face still twinkled

THE PETER OWEN ANTHOLOGY

with mischief, and a flash of ill-temper gleamed in his eyes.

She looked him up and down stealthily and remarked: 'So we're new here, are we? Never been out in a boat all this year, by what I can see.'

Aurelio broke in: 'He looks a lot better with an oar in his hand. Then he'd beat all those family men you've tipped into the Po. Any oar! Even a bit of wood!'

'I've never seen him rowing past here though. By the look of him, I'd say the poor soul was at his last gasp after three months of sciatica. Glad to get a bit of fresh air again, eh?'

The young man screwed up his mouth and spat on the ground. Without turning round he asked his companion, out of the corner of his mouth, 'Got everything?'

Aurelio slipped behind the curtain and brought out a small case that he put into the first punt. Then he jumped aboard and stood with his legs wide apart, rocking the little boat to work it free of the others and creating tumultuous repercussions all along the line.

'It's quite ready,' the old woman cried, bringing along a paddle and a punt pole with an iron rim. 'I baled out just now, after those other two got me out of bed. All you've got to do is get in,' and with a powerful sweep of her arm she swung out the heavy pole.

'Let's hope so,' Aurelio replied.

The old woman turned with a grin to Moro, who was standing there doing nothing, and eyed him again, curiously, from head to foot. To Aurelio she said: 'Your friend still looks bleary eyed. Watch out! If you run into a bridge there'll be damages to pay.'

'You be careful nobody runs into you,' Moro retorted. He clambered awkwardly into the boat, making Aurelio nearly lose his balance. 'Hand over that paddle,' he said coldly as he turned round, 'and cast off.'

The old woman did as he told her. Aurelio looked up at the sky. By now the pink clouds had gone. Standing in the stern, Aurelio thrust the pole straight down and forced the boat out with all the power of his wrists from among the others until it swung free as the current caught it. 'Cheerio,' the old woman muttered, but neither man made any reply and she went back to the bathing-hut.

Aurelio, in his black swimsuit, kept raising and lowering the pole, probing the bottom, bending forward to exert his utmost strength against the pressure of the water. He looked steadily ahead at the smooth, shining stream, screwing up his eyes against the glare. He came out into the sunlight.

Moro was lying in the bottom of the boat, filling it completely, his hairy legs dangling over the sides. He raised his hand to shade his eyes.

'Isn't the sunshine grand, Moro?'

'It's grand to see it from here,' Moro muttered.

'It's the same everywhere,' Aurelio replied. 'But it won't be so bright for long, this morning. Look at those clouds coming up.'

'The worst of it is, when you're inside, all the sun does is heat your cell. It's not just sunshine, it's a blazing furnace.'

'Then in winter it keeps you warm.'

'In winter you freeze and you can't say a thing. But the worst thing is that in summer, when there's a sun like this, you've got to stick it out in jacket and trousers. Take your jacket off? No, sir, not on your life! Take off your jacket when they let you out in the exercise yard? You can't. Why not? You just can't.'

'It's the same for soldiers, anyway.'

'No, this was worse. They shut a man up just so as to make him walk round the dustbins.'

Aurelio, bending forward to thrust in the pole, laughed down into Moro's face. Moro, raising his hand and screwing up his eyes, grinned back at him.

Covering his eyes again, Moro went on: 'Once a man's in prison it means he's a bad lot. Nobody wants no-goods like us. They tell us we must change our way of life and meantime they keep us shut up like rabbits. If we're to change our way of living they should let us get on with it, turn us loose at once. Instead, no. You've got to stay there two, three, ten years, depending on what your record says; turn yellow, green, grey – that's the only change in life you'll get. D'you know that where I was there was a man serving twenty years? He looked like my grandfather did when he was dead, yet he was only forty. Murder. All because he'd had a drop too much.'

'Still, some fools let themselves be caught when they shouldn't,' said Aurelio as he bent forward again.

Moro started up to sit facing Aurelio. 'But what if justice is worse than we are?' he exclaimed. 'Why don't they kill a man right off if they catch him at it? Or, if he's just picking pockets, give him a sound thrashing, like men? Then we'd soon see who had the best of it. It's a priests' trick to keep a man shut up for years. Don't you think so?'

'But all they gave you was a year and a half.'

'A year's nothing. It's the days that are so long.'

'You didn't used to be so dim, Moro. You haven't got the prison food out of your system yet. It's upset your stomach and you look scared stiff.'

Moro rummaged in the attaché-case and brought out a cigarette. The pale little flame in the sunshine showed up the pale little hollows in his drawn cheeks. He tossed the match away.

Aurelio said: 'What you ought to be doing is learning a bit more sense. Take care where you operate another time. Who ever heard of a stick-up in broad daylight? You're no good at that sort of job, anyway.'

'I'm all right in a boat, though,' Moro exclaimed, jumping to his feet so suddenly that Aurelio almost over-balanced. 'Give me that pole.'

Cautiously Aurelio edged over to Moro's side and passed him the pole. Then he sat down and tried to smoke. Moro, his cigarette twisted between his lips, felt for the bottom and made his first thrust, then slowly straightened up.

Bianca raised her dripping paddle and the punt glided forward under the trees into the still water. 'The sunshine's gone,' Clara grumbled.

Bianca, clenching her teeth, threw herself down on the bank and looked around. 'It's that cloud making the water seem dark,' she said. 'If the sun comes out again it will be all silvery.'

'Is it going to rain?'

'I don't think so, but even if it does, we're here to go swimming.'

'You're a real river-girl,' Clara murmured, and Bianca looked away, determined not to lose her temper at the lazy mockery in her friend's eyes.

Clara remarked: 'Why ever didn't you notice how low the swallows are flying over the Po?'

Bianca swung round to look at the river. Through the little opening where they had come in she could see the current running swiftly past in a belt of sunlight. Out in mid-stream a dredger was floating, moored to a slanting cable and rocking as the water rippled round it. It was quite deserted.

'That's where we can go if it rains. I've never been on board a dredger.'

'There isn't a soul about,' Clara said. 'Once those poor sand-grubbers have gone home – and seeing they spend their life on the water they could at least wash themselves – the river is a desert. Anyone could die – or be born – here and nobody would know. It's like some bygone civilization.' She leaned over the side of the boat and added: 'Except for all those sardine tins and broken jars. They strike a different note. Actually I don't think much of your river.'

Clara's supple body in its tight-fitting yellow bathing costume threw back a pale reflection as she leaned over the greenish water. Bianca watched her almost against her will, making no reply. But then she smiled. Clara was gazing at her own face in the water and rubbing the corner of her eye with one finger. 'So any mirror's enough to put the fair lady

Clara in a better humour,' Bianca mocked, conscious that her voice was shaking uncontrollably.

'Taking one mirror with another, I prefer my own. At least in that one I don't see a shoal of little fish shooting out of my mouth, and it doesn't make me look drunk. Nor does it give me a halo from a sunken bowl.'

Involuntarily, Bianca's fists clenched, but she controlled herself, stretching out her arms and relaxing her cramped fingers. At ease again, she turned her head, letting her eyes wander over the sky and the trees on the bank. Beyond their trunks stretched a pleasant beach, shining against a mass of cloud. 'I didn't promise you the River Amazon,' she said good-humouredly, 'but that's what we'll get if it rains. Why take shelter, anyway? What can be lovelier than a morning storm?'

'Listen, dear. If you want to have a swim, get on with it. It's going to pour any minute and my costume isn't meant to get wet.'

'I want to see you get in.'

'Bianca! Is that why you've brought me all up here? For me to jump into that black water and get covered with filthy mud and bitten by crocodiles? Bianca! I have pretty skin and it needs looking after. It's a good thing that sun you're so fond of has been kind and respectful to a poor blonde without much on.'

'Stupid,' Bianca replied with a shrug. 'This life would do you good, make you stronger and more confident.'

'But I'm strong already. Too strong and self-reliant, really. What I need is the opposite. It's cost me one love affair, being so strong.'

Bianca bent down to undo her canvas shoes, looking sideways at Clara and listening as she went on: 'It never does to show people you're strong and self-reliant. They're only too ready to knock it out of you.'

'Why don't you give up this aimless way of life?' Bianca asked with a smile.

'It isn't as dull as some, you know.'

'I see,' Bianca murmured softly, feeling in her bag for her rubber bathing-cap.

When she stood ready she turned to Clara, who lay at full length in the bottom of the boat grinning up at her. 'So you really aren't coming?' she asked.

'You go, and come back in triumph. I'll give you a clap.'

'Won't you at least swim in here? I'll hold you up.'

'My precious, you're too silly for words. One plays that game with men, not with another girl. Off you go, and don't break your neck.'

Bianca shivered as she entered the water, and waded with uncertain steps towards the opening. Then she clenched her teeth and dived. The water was not cold. Over here in mid-stream the dredger was twinkling in the sun. She stood up again with the water up to her waist, and felt the wind cold on her shoulders.

She passed the ripples swirling by the opening and saw the current running strongly ahead. The bottom was deeper now. She glanced over her shoulder at the surface of the water, the low banks, the boat, the vague blur of trees, then stretched herself in a powerful swimming stroke. Suddenly she was out into the tumbling current. She turned up-stream from the dredger, swimming straight towards the hill now veiled by the sun and clouds, and plunging her face into the dark gurgling water, catching her breath as best she could in the pauses between her arm strokes. Her progress across the current threatened to break her rhythm at any moment and she could see nothing but flashing drops of spray. Exhausted by her efforts to breathe she dropped her head for the last time and suddenly saw the water below the surface made transparent by diffused sunlight. She raised her head. The dredger was only a few yards away.

Bianca worked her way around the rocking hull, looking for somewhere to hold on. A shadow ran across the water. The last of the sunshine had gone. The chill wind blew stronger.

Bianca pulled herself up, scraping her knee on the

vessel's side. The metal superstructure with its pulleys and sand-encrusted gratings took up most of the space, leaving only a narrow ledge all round. Unsteadily she made her way along it and came to a hut of rough boards tucked in among the machinery. It had an earthy floor and a pile of folded sacks in one corner. In the middle, the deck was cut away, leaving an empty space of bubbling black water – the river itself. A chain of buckets hung down into it from an opening dimly visible in the roof high above.

Bianca went outside again to watch the current rushing out from below the hull, and her eyes opened in wide amazement at the flood pouring down towards the weir, broken by stones and torn branches. She reflected that only an hour earlier they had been punting on the river, and she remembered Clara.

She ran to the side of the dredger and looked for the little break in the woods where they had landed. At first she saw nothing but the low, green bank, distant and motionless under the swaying trees. Then, behind a spit of land, she caught sight of Clara's light-coloured costume. She was standing waving the paddle, shouting shrilly and pointing at the sky.

'There's shelter here,' Bianca yelled. 'It's safe enough.'

Apparently Clara heard, for she waved her hand and disappeared behind the little promontory. The first thunder rumbled in the distance. Nervously, Bianca whipped off her rubber cap. Terrifying clouds were piling up, and a sudden bright flash of lightning darted across the sky. Bianca pressed her hands on the hull and stared down at the water swirling and foaming below her. The thunder did not come for a moment and she started shouting: 'Clara, it's . . .'

There came a low roar that gradually grew louder and louder, echoing among the hills and swelling like the noise of a landslide until it crashed in the distance and died away with a dull reverberation. Bianca flushed as her fears left her. It was raining in the city, for certain. Down there in the valley the sky looked terrible.

'Clara, it's all right here. I'm coming to fetch you.' Cold wind-squalls blowing up the river whistled round the dredger, making it swing on its mooring. 'Where on earth has she got to, the silly girl!' Bianca muttered to herself, peering at the low bank and the tall trees swaying wildly against the clear streak of the horizon.

Then she saw the boat coming out of the opening with Clara in it, frenziedly straining with the paddle and raising great splashes of foam. But once out in the current she lost course, caught up in the eddies and gusts of wind.

'Careful!' Bianca yelled. 'You'll end up over the weir!' and she ran along the hull, watching the boat being swept inexorably downstream. Then Clara stood up. (The thought flashed into Bianca's mind that she looked just like a canary.) She seized the heavy, iron-rimmed pole and leaned forward to thrust it in over the stern. The punt swung further downstream. Clara was gripping the pole with all her might, holding it upright and trying to find the bottom. There was no bottom, and every time she tried to probe for it the current drove the punt hard against the pole, wrenching her wrists painfully. 'Idiot!' Bianca howled, almost beside herself. 'Go sideways! Put that pole down. Use the paddle!'

She was frantically pulling on her cap again when she heard a scream. Clara had disappeared. She had fallen into the water behind the punt. A patch of wild splashing in the wake of the boat showed where she was struggling.

Bianca dived in, at the same moment almost blinded by a lightning flash. Only in the water could she feel safe. She swam desperately, head down, seeing nothing, hearing nothing, not even the thunder clap. For the moment she was not thinking of Clara. She was straining every nerve to reach the punt and salvage the pole. Then she could save Clara.

Her arm bumped against the pole. Looking round through the spray, she could see something yellow splashing about some distance away; in the other direction, in the grip of the current, she saw the empty punt. 'Without the boat I'll never manage to pull her out' flashed through her mind, and pushing the pole ahead of her she made for the punt. She reached it and threw in the pole. Heaving herself over the side, out of the rushing water, almost tore her shoulders apart, but at last she rolled in, bruised all over, and seized the paddle. When she turned round there was no longer any sign of Clara. Only then did she notice it was raining in torrents, great blasts that cut furrows in the surface of the river. Clouds of fine spray like smoke billowed everywhere and her back began to tingle, stung by the violence of the downpour.

Clara was no longer there. Bianca tossed her head to free her eyes from the matted hair that was blinding her. She had lost her cap, and had to run her fingers through her hair before she could push it away. A wild yell burst from her: 'Clara!'

All around her the water boiled, its surface unbroken. Steering the boat with the paddle and holding it steady against the current she peered into the swirling flood, trying to find the place where Clara had disappeared. Millions of tiny bubbles spread a layer of pale foam between the water and the air. Through the raindrops Bianca looked for the bank, but everything had vanished. All she could see was a vague outline. She was alone on the river.

Plying the paddle frenziedly she made some headway against the current, thankful to be still afloat, heedless of her direction. Then, through the hair still hanging over her eyes, she noticed she was level with a certain tall tree growing on the bank. Her teeth chattering with fright, she jumped to her feet in the drenching rain and put down the paddle. 'She called me a "river girl",' she murmured breathlessly and plunged in, hurting her foot badly.

Under the surface she found a great calm. The dense mass of water deadened every sound, made every effort seem remote and pointless. She strained her eyes in the darkness and groped about with her hands, but she saw nothing and felt nothing except the weight of the water. When she surfaced she was surprised by the light and the rain. She had quite forgotten them. The punt was not far away. She turned and dived again, probing about until her ears were buzzing and her arm strokes grew weak. She surfaced again and swam to the boat, clinging to it with her whole body and tearing her costume as she clambered in.

Ankle-deep in water, she picked up the paddle again and looked around her, uncertain what to do. Then her heart leapt. There in the mist was another boat with two men in it, creeping along the opposite bank and making straight for the dredger.

Bianca jumped to her feet and started shouting, waving the paddle. The warm rain splashed into her mouth. The men did not turn. 'Over here!' she yelled, loud enough to split her throat. She almost added: 'Help!', but refrained. Her bag was floating in the bottom of the punt. She pulled out a towel and waved it, still shouting.

The men were now level with the dredger and paddled round, looking up at it. As Bianca watched, one of them jumped aboard it and the other, bending forward in the rain, handed up a rope. She glanced at the foaming current as it swept past, loaded with mud, then, clenching her teeth, she turned the boat towards the dredger and paddled furiously.

Out of the rain her half-drowned head came level with the hull. 'Oh!' Aurelio was saying as he threw himself down on the sacks, 'Look at the state we're in!' Moro, standing naked at the back of the hut, wringing out his swimming trunks, did not turn.

'Here's a woman!' Aurelio exclaimed.

She clutched the rail with both hands and the little boat slid from under her feet. 'A girl's been drowned,' she cried shrilly. 'Come and help me.'

Aurelio ran forward to give her a hand. 'If you don't come aboard, you'll be drowned, too,' he cried. 'Moro, come and help!'

The girl, her hand in Aurelio's, looked back and forth

from him to the river. She was steaming like a horse; her sunburnt skin looked sodden and lifeless; her arms and legs were covered with scratches.

'A friend of mine's been drowned,' she cried. 'I've got to find her. I've been calling for ages.'

'Even the fishes would drown on a day like this,' said Moro in the darkness of the hut, holding his trunks to shield his hairy stomach.

'Jump in! Jump in,' Aurelio urged again. 'You're over the worst. If it was all that time ago, she's dead by now. Where did it happen?'

'Down there,' the girl sobbed, pointing to the current and trying to release her other hand. 'Over there.'

'She went under?'

'D'you expect people to drown in the air?' Moro sneered in the background.

'Jump in,' said Aurelio. 'Too much water is bad for anyone. There's a hut here. Your boat's waterlogged already.'

Moro came forward with his costume draped around him. 'Where does she say it happened?' he asked.

'Over there. Just beyond the Sangone.' She turned her eyes in that direction and the drops fell from her matted hair like a flood of tears.

'Come on into shelter,' Aurelio persisted, pulling her by the arm. 'If that's where she went down, the current won't carry her beyond the weir. We know where to find her. Was she the same age as you?'

'Could she swim?' Moro added.

'Can you swim yourself?' the girl asked sharply.

Moro flung himself down on a seat at the edge of the hut, his trunks between his thighs. Aurelio was still bending over the side trying to pull the girl in, and Moro kicked him on the ankle. 'Don't you see?' he said out of the corner of his mouth. 'These are the girls from the landing-stage. My dear bathing beauty,' he went on, 'we can swim a lot better than people like you who come here to act the fool when other folk are working, but we swim in water, not in rain.

We'll see about that later, if you like. But for the present, we'll let it rain. Leave her to get out of it by herself.'

Aurelio, uncertain what to do, relaxed his hold and went back into the hut, the water dripping from him. Slowly the boat drifted backwards. The girl stood there for a moment, raising her shoulder to rub her cheek. Then she leaned forward, picked up the paddle and brought the punt alongside the dredger again.

Without a word she pulled herself up on the hull, holding the boat's mooring chain between her teeth. Then she turned her back and crouched forward to thread the chain through a ring in the hull. As she did so, she found that her black costume was split all down the left side and torn at the hem on her thigh. Her white flesh gleamed through the holes, very different from the bronzed skin of her legs and shoulders.

Having secured the chain, she leaned forward to take her bag from the boat. Aurelio's eyes followed the play of her pale skin under her torn costume. Without looking at him, the girl staggered to her feet – she was short and dark, like him – and put down her sodden bag inside the hut. Then she sat down under the shelter, apart from the other two, her knees against her chest. She rested her elbows on them and took her cheeks in her hands, sitting very still and staring at the rain.

The whole dredger quivered and rocked as the current washed past it. Down from the opening in the roof of the hut where the pulley-chains ran came cold blasts that cut into their backs. Aurelio, crouching on his sacks, looked at Moro's long, bare spine and the girl's shoulders, shining against the background of the rain.

'Moro,' he said suddenly, breaking the silence, 'cover up your seat, or this draught'll give you a chill.'

Moro grinned across at him. 'It's not proper to put on one's trousers in the presence of a young lady.'

'D'you think you're so handsome? Young ladies don't look.'

'They're too well brought up to say anything.'

Aurelio stuffed one hand into the little case lying on the sacks. 'Want a cigarette?'

'If they're not soaked, too.'

Aurelio stood up and held out the packet to Moro, taking one out with his lips at the same time. Then he turned to the girl and offered her one. 'Let's have a smoke on it,' he said. She made no response but still sat motionless, staring at the rain.

'Thanks very much, but I don't smoke,' he prompted her as he went back to the sacks and struck a match.

'You see what women are like,' Moro told him, trying in vain to strike a match in his turn. 'The whole world at their beck and call. Acting so foolhardy and running into danger when they haven't any idea what the Po can be like. When a man reasons with them they spit at his feet and ask him if he can swim. Somebody who can really swim doesn't let anyone drown. What'll you bet, Aurelio, that the other girl couldn't swim, either?'

Irritably, Aurelio threw away his cigarette and wandered restlessly round the hut, trying out the chain that held the buckets. He thrust his hand inside his costume to rub his shivering chest and finally came to sit beside the girl at the front of the hut. Moro was watching her out of the corner of his eye. Like her, Aurelio pulled his knees against his chest and rested his cheeks on his hands. 'Pretty girls don't cry,' he told her with a wink.

She flushed, jumped to her feet and turned to go inside, but Aurelio held her by the arm and tried to pull her back. Then he let her go. 'All right, all right,' he said. 'We know each other. At least I know your friend was a blonde.'

The girl stared at him a moment with blazing eyes. 'I told you myself,' she muttered as she ran inside. Then she swung round in the gloom and asked him: 'How did you manage to find out that?'

'I'll tell you, if you tell me your name,' Aurelio smiled as he rose to his feet.

'It's Piccone,' she answered quickly. 'So what?'

Moro burst out laughing and slapped his thigh.

'Your own name,' Aurelio persisted, still smiling. 'What does your surname matter to me?'

She stood still a moment, disconcerted. Then her whole face flamed red and distorted, as if he had struck her across the mouth.

Suddenly an oath burst from Moro. He had jumped up hurriedly and his trunks had fallen overboard. Dropping to his knees he stretched his arm down but failed to reach them. Then, naked as he was, he leapt into the girl's boat with a great splash and fished them out, dripping wet. He climbed up again, still uncovered. 'Blast! They were practically dry,' he exclaimed as he threw them down in a corner and stalked into the hut.

The girl watched him come, her eyes fixed on his face. Without glancing aside, he said, from the corner of his mouth: 'Both those boats are full of water. Go and bale them out, Aurelio.' The girl backed away.

'Where have we seen the blonde, Miss Piccone?' Moro sneered, his face close to hers. 'The dead float, you fool! They can swim much better than you or me. D'you know where that blonde is now?' Moro's voice sank to a chilling whisper. The girl could see his teeth. 'She's here behind you, in this patch of water. Her eyes are open and her nails all broken. She's calling you, raising her hand. She's going to grab you!'

Terrified, the girl crouched down on the sacks. Moro laughed over her shoulders. 'Silly fool,' he said, gripping her sides with his hands.

Aurelio shook him by the shoulder. 'You can't do things like that, you great lout. You're only frightening her. D'you think you're still in prison? I was the one who helped her. It's my affair.'

The girl struggled to her knees. Moro thrust her down again with his fist in her neck and his shin in the small of her back. Suddenly he turned his tense, fleshless face to Aurelio and said with a grin, 'Go and bale out those punts, I tell you. This Piccone girl has seen me; she's fallen for me; she wants me.'

'You shouldn't have got stripped. It isn't fair.'

'Sure,' Moro retorted, swaying as the girl struggled beneath him. 'I don't want any of your nonsense. Go and bale out the punts. They're sinking.'

The girl collapsed on the sacks so suddenly that Moro almost fell on top of her. Her limp body in its torn black costume lay white and slack.

'You've killed her!' Aurelio cried.

'They're like cats. They squeal if you only hold them under water.'

Out in the rain again, Aurelio stared at the current instead of seeing to the boats, watching it foaming, yellow with mud, under the water streaming from the sky. Eddies formed, swirled away and formed again round the dredger as it swung and rolled in the fierce grip of the flood, all its metal parts clanking noisily. Now and then a broken oar flashed past, glimpsed for an instant before it rolled under again. Over in the valley, everything looked vague and indistinct; the masses of trees on the deserted banks seemed in a different world. One could guess how the water must be roaring and foaming over the rapids by the weir.

Both punts were full. The one the girl had brought was half submerged. Aurelio glanced sideways at the dripping entrance to the hut, then threw himself forward and picked up a short end of wood floating in the boat. Blinded by the rain, he leaned out from the hull and made a few aimless movements with it. Then he drew back again as heavy breathing and a long, low groan reached him from the hut, and the sound of material being ripped. He looked round quickly and glimpsed in the gloom a pale, shapeless mass of struggling bodies.

He sat down again on the hull, stretching out his brown legs in the rain and staring at the punt as it rocked gently. The water inside it was clear, compared with the river, and the varnished bottom planking shone through. The iron-rimmed pole was still there. The paddle had been washed away.

He heard Moro cursing, but would not turn round. He heard sounds of a struggle and a long moan. Then, silence except for the rain.

Aurelio unbuttoned his swimsuit at the shoulder and rolled it down to his waist. He examined his chest as he breathed in and out. The cold air tasted of mud and leaves. Then he tried to purse up his lips and whistle a tune, but no sound came out.

'Aurelio! Quick!' Moro's hoarse voice broke the silence. 'Here's another one dead!'

Aurelio sprang up. Moro was sitting at the back of the hut, clutching his knees against his chest. Aurelio barely had time to glimpse the girl lying at full length before she leapt to her feet, deathly white in spite of great black bruises, her costume in tatters. She fled across the dark space, pushed Aurelio aside and fell into the water.

Aurelio had knocked his knee against the planks but he recovered his balance and turned round as a roar of laughter from Moro made his ears ring.

'She's done it on you! See! That's women for you!'

The girl was already some way off, swimming spasmodically with great splashes, half out of the water. Aurelio jumped into the boat, almost capsizing it. It took him a moment or two to cast off.

'It's no good,' Moro said, coming up beside him. 'I told you to bale out. You won't do it now in the time. You've let her get away.'

Aurelio would have thrown himself into the water in his frenzy, but Moro held him back. 'She won't get far. A woman's worn out when I've finished with her. Watch!'

The girl was rolling helplessly in the current, incapable of guiding herself, and ending up in mid-stream, splashing feebly and drifting rapidly towards the weir. 'So she can't swim,' said Moro. 'Still, I gave her a good lesson.'

'She's drowning,' Aurelio cried, 'and I . . .'

'Come back in the shadow,' Moro urged, pulling him by the arm. 'Have you gone crazy? It couldn't be better. She left us of her own free will. Besides, girls like her always talk.'

Aurelio had lost sight of that black speck and stood trembling, straining his eyes.

'Now I'll have a smoke. Be glad to,' Moro said as he went back inside. When, a few minutes later, Aurelio joined him and threw himself down on the sacks, Moro went on curtly: 'Have a cigarette. Never mind. You shall do it first another time.'

Title story from the collection *Summer Storm*, translated from the Italian by A. E. Murch

The Monkey Grammarian

OCTAVIO PAZ

The body of Splendor as it divides, disperses, dissipates itself in my body as it divides, disperses, dissipates itself in the body of Splendor:

breathing, warmth, outline, bulk that beneath the pressure of my fingertips slowly ceases to be a confusion of pulses and gathers itself together and reunites with itself,

vibrations, waves that strike my closed eyelids as the street lamps go out and dawn staggers through the city:

the body of Splendor before my eyes that gaze down on her as she lies between the sheets as I walk toward her in the dawn in the green light filtering through the enormous leaves of a banana tree onto an ocher footpath to Galta that leads me to this page where the body of Splendor lies between the sheets as I write on this page and as I read what I write,

an ocher footpath that suddenly starts walking, a river of burned waters seeking its path between the sheets, Splendor rises from the bed and walks about in the shadowy light of the room with staggering steps as the street lamps of the city go out:

she is searching for something, the dawn is searching for something, the young woman halts and looks at me: a squirrel gaze, a dawn gaze that lingers amid the leaves of the banyan tree along the ocher path that leads from Galta to this page, a gaze that is a well to be drunk from, a gaze in which I write the word reconciliation:

Splendor is this page, that which separates (liberates)

177

and weaves together (reconciles) the various parts that compose it,

that which (the one who) is there, at the end of what I say, at the end of this page, and appears here as this phrase is uttered, as it dissipates,

the act inscribed on this page and the bodies (the phrases) that as they embrace give form to this act, this body:

the liturgical sequence and the dissipation of all rites through the double profanation (yours and mine), the reconciliation/liberation, of writing and reading

Cambridge, England, summer 1970

Chapter 29 from *The Monkey Grammarian*, translated from the Spanish by Helen R. Lane

The eighteenth-century palace of Galta from *The Monkey Grammarian*,
Octavio Paz. The photograph is by Eusebio Rojas

Undine
Gyofukuki

OSAMU DAZAI

The literal title of this tale, 'An Account of Taking on the Guise of a Fish,' has been altered to 'Undine' in the interests of euphony. Undine figures in Western mythology as a female water spirit who can become human by marrying a man and bearing a child. (Translator's note)

I

In the far north of Honshu there's a row of low hills known as the Bonju Range. Only three or four hundred meters high at best, these hills don't appear on an ordinary map.

Long ago the entire area was apparently under the sea, and people in the region still say that the hero Yoshitsune once came here by boat. It happened after he had gone into hiding and was fleeing northward toward the shores of faraway Ezo. His boat ran aground – there's a square patch of red soil some ten meters across on a low tree-covered hill midway along the range that shows where he landed.

They call this particular place Bald Horse Hill. That's because, from the village below, the patch of red soil is supposed to resemble a galloping horse. In fact it's more like an old man's profile.

Bald Horse Hill is also famous hereabouts for its scenery. A stream emerges from behind the hill and flows past the village and its twenty or thirty homes. Several miles up this stream a waterfall descends from a cliff. The waterfall is one hundred feet high and looks very white.

The trees covering this hill begin to change color at the end of summer. The leaves are beautiful in the autumn, and people come from the provincial towns to view them, enlivening even this remote place for a time. At the foot of the falls there is a small tea stand to serve them.

Just as the season was getting underway this year, a death occurred at the falls – an accidental death, though, and not a suicide. The victim was a student from the city with a pale complexion. He had come, as others occasionally do, to collect some of the rare ferns that grow here.

The pool below the falls is surrounded almost entirely by high cliffs. A narrow gap opens to the west, and here the water rushes against the rocks and pours out into the stream. The ferns grow in patches down the cliffs, moistened by the constant spray and quivering in the roar of the waters.

The student had been scaling one of the cliffs. It was afternoon, and the early autumn sun still shone overhead. When he was halfway up, a rock the size of a man's head suddenly gave way beneath his foot, and he fell as though he had been torn away from the cliff. On the way down he got snared by the branch of an aging tree. But the branch snapped, and he was sent plummeting into the pool below with a horrible splash.

Several people nearby witnessed the fall. The girl who looked after the tea stand – she was going on fourteen – saw it best.

She watched him sink far into the pool and then float up until his body rose halfway above the surface. At that moment his eyes were shut, his mouth was slightly open.

His blue shirt was torn in places while the collector's box still hung from his shoulder.

The next moment he was again sucked down – all the way to the bottom.

II

On clear days from late spring until well into autumn, columns of white smoke can be seen even from faraway rising over Bald Horse Hill. The sap runs abundantly then, and the trees are just right for producing charcoal. So the charcoal-makers work hard at their kilns during this period.

There are ten or so huts on Bald Horse Hill, each with a kiln. One of the kilns is located near the waterfall, off by itself. The other charcoal-makers are from this area, while the man working this kiln comes from a distant part of the country. The girl who runs the tea stand is the man's daughter. Named Suwa, she lives alone with her father throughout the year.

Two years ago, when Suwa was twelve, her father set up the little stand with logs and a reed screen. He also arranged a number of things on the shelves for her to sell – lemonade and crackers, rice jelly, and all sorts of sweet candies.

With summer approaching once again and people beginning to come around, Suwa's father would assemble the stand. He would then carry the provisions there every morning in a basket, his daughter skipping along behind him in her bare feet. Upon reaching the site, he would soon go back to the hut and his own kiln, leaving Suwa there all alone.

If she caught even a glimpse of any sightseers, Suwa would call out the greeting her father had taught her – 'Hello! Please stop in for a while.' But the roaring falls drowned out her sweet voice, and she could seldom catch anyone's attention. In a whole day she could not even take in fifty sen.

Her father would return at dusk, his entire body black as charcoal.

'How much did you get?' he'd ask.

'Nothing.'

'Too bad,' he would mutter, as if it didn't much matter. After looking up at the falls, he would place the sweets back in the basket. And then they would go back to the hut.

It went on like this day after day until the frost came.

Suwa's father could leave her alone at the tea stand without having to worry. Since she had grown up among these hills, she wasn't going to lose her footing on a rock and plunge into the waterfall pool. In fact, when the weather was good, she would take off her clothes, dive into the pool, and swim up close to the falls. If she noticed someone while she was swimming, she would toss her short brown hair from her forehead with one hand and then cry out, 'Hello! Please stop in for a while.'

When it rained, Suwa would crawl under a straw mat in the corner and take a nap. A large oak grew out over the tea stand, its abundant leaves providing shelter from the rain.

Suwa would gaze up at the thundering falls and imagine that the water would eventually run out. She also wondered why the waterfall always took the same shape.

Lately her thoughts had deepened.

She could now tell that the waterfall didn't always keep the same shape. In fact the varying width and the changing pattern of the spray made one dizzy. Finally the billowing at the crest made her realize that the falls was more clouds of mist than streams of water. Besides, she knew that water itself could never be so white.

One day Suwa lingered dreamily beside the falls. As the sky became overcast and the early autumn wind reddened her cheeks and made them smart, she remembered the tale her father had told her some time ago. He had held her in his lap then, while keeping an eye on the kiln.

The story concerned two brothers, Saburō and Hachirō, both of whom worked as woodcutters. Hachirō, the younger brother, had caught some trout in a mountain stream and had brought them back home. Before Saburō returned from the mountains, Hachirō grilled one of the trout and ate it. The fish tasted good, so he ate two or three more of them. After that, he couldn't stop until he had eaten the entire catch. He was thirsty now – so thirsty that he drank all the water in the well. Then he ran to the river at the edge of the village and kept on drinking. Scales suddenly spread out over his body. By the time his brother came running back, Hachirō had become a great serpent and was swimming in the river.

'Hachirō! What is it?' Saburō called out.

Shedding tears, the serpent called back from out in the river. 'Ah, Saburō!'

Weeping and wailing, the two brothers called back and forth, one from the bank and the other from the river – 'Ah, Hachirō!' 'Ah, Saburō!' Unfortunately there was nothing that could be done.

This tale had so moved Suwa that she had put her father's charcoal-blackened finger into her small mouth and wept.

Coming out of her reverie, she gazed at the falls in wonder. The water seemed to murmur – 'Ah, Hachirō! Ah, Saburō! Ah, Hachirō!'

Her father, pushing the leaves aside, emerged from the red ivy that hung along the cliff.

'How much did you sell, Suwa?'

Her nose glistened with spray from the falls. She rubbed it without making any reply. Silently her father gathered up the things.

They headed home, pushing through the bamboo grass that overgrew the mountain road. Before they had covered the quarter mile back, Suwa's father said, 'Maybe you should quit now.' He shifted the basket from his right hand to his left, the lemonade bottles clinking against one another. 'It's getting cold,' he went on, 'and no one's coming any more.'

As the sunlight faded, the only sound was that of the wind. Once in a while the leaves falling from the oak or fir trees would strike against the father and daughter like sharp hailstones.

'Papa,' Suwa called out from behind, 'what are you living for?'

The huge shoulders merely shrugged. Then Suwa's father looked closely into his daughter's determined face and muttered, 'Nothing, I guess.'

Suwa bit off part of the long grass leaf she was holding.

'You're better off dead, then.'

His hand flew up – he would teach her some respect! Then, hesitantly, he lowered it. His daughter had been on edge for some time now. He realized that she was getting to be a woman and he must leave her be.

'All right,' he conceded, 'all right.'

Stupid! That's what this listless reply was – stupid! Suwa spat out bits of the leaf. 'Fool!' she screamed. 'You're a fool!'

III

The Festival of the Dead* was over, and the tea stand had been taken down for the winter. For Suwa this was the worst time of the year.

Every fourth day or so her father would hoist a bag of charcoal onto his shoulders and set off for the market. There were men for hire who did this sort of work, but he could not afford the fifteen or twenty sen they would charge. Leaving Suwa all alone, he would carry the load himself to the village below the hill.

---

* Traditional Buddhist feast observed in July or August.

When the weather was good, Suwa would hunt mushrooms while her father was gone. After all, the charcoal would not bring in enough for them to live on, even when it sold for five or six sen a bag. So Suwa had to pick mushrooms for her father to sell as well.

The moist, pea-shaped *nameko* would fetch a good price. They grew in clusters on decaying logs among clumps of fern. Each time Suwa saw moss on the logs, she thought of the only friend she had ever had. She liked to sprinkle the moss on top of her mushroom-filled basket and head for home.

Whenever her father sold the charcoal or mushrooms for a good price, he would return with saké on his breath. Once in a while he would bring back a paper purse or some other gift for Suwa.

One day a raging wind blew about the hill from early morning, causing the straw mats that served as curtains to swing back and forth within the hut. Suwa's father had gone down to the village at dawn.

She decided to stay inside today and arrange her hair, an unusual thing for her to do. When she had finished tying up her curls in a paper ribbon patterned with waves, a present that her father had given her, Suwa stoked the fire and sat down to await his return. Now and then the call of a wild animal could be heard, along with the rustling of leaves.

After the sun went down, Suwa prepared her supper. It was fried bean paste over brown rice, and she ate it all alone.

As the night deepened, the wind died down and the weather turned cold. An unearthly quiet settled upon the hill, the kind of quiet in which wondrous events are bound to happen. Suwa heard all sorts of things – *tengu* demons* toppling the forest trees, someone right outside the hut

---

* A demon of grotesque appearance. The *tengu* derives from a mountain god associated with large trees, and its evil doings include the abduction of children.

swishing adzuki beans* in fresh water. She even caught the clear echo of a hermit's laughter in the distance.

Tired of waiting for her father, Suwa wrapped herself in a straw quilt and lay down by the hearth. As she dozed, a creature occasionally lifted the straw mat hanging in the doorway and peeked in. Thinking that this was a hermit from the mountains, Suwa pretended to be fast asleep.

In the glow of the dying fire, something else could just be made out fluttering through the entrance onto the dirt floor. Snow – the first of the season! Suwa was elated, even as she appeared to dream.

Pain. The heavy body almost numbed her. Then she smelled the reeking breath.

'Fool!' she screamed. Blindly she fled outside.

Snow! Whirling this way and that, it struck her right in the face. She sat down, her hair and dress already covered with flakes. Then she got up and trudged ahead, her shoulders heaving as she gasped for breath. She walked on and on, her clothes whipping about in the gale.

The sound of the falls grew steadily louder. On she marched, wiping her nose over and over with the palm of her hand. Now the roar of the falls was almost at her feet.

There was a narrow gap among the wintry, moaning trees. She leapt through it, murmuring one word.

'Papa.'

IV

When she came to, it was dim and shadowy all over. She sensed the rumbling of the waterfall far above. Her body, vibrating with the sound, felt chilled to the bone.

---

* The red color of adzuki beans is considered auspicious, and they are often served on happy occasions.

Ah, the bottom of the waterfall pool. With that realization she felt refreshed and clean.

She stretched her legs, sliding ahead without a sound. Her nose nearly bumped against the edge of a rock.

Serpent!

Yes, she had turned into a serpent. How fortunate that she could never again go back to the hut. Telling herself these things, she tried moving her chin whiskers in a circle.

In fact, she was only a small carp. Her tiny mouth nibbled at the water while the wart on her nose wiggled back and forth.

The carp then swam about in the pool, near the deep basin beneath the waterfall. Moving her pectoral fins, she rose close to the surface, then suddenly dove, her tail thrashing hard.

She chased after tiny shrimp in the water, hid in the reeds along the bank, and tugged at the moss growing upon a rock's edge.

Then the carp lay still. Once in a while the pectoral fins twitched ever so slightly. It remained this way for a time, as if in contemplation.

Then, with a twisting motion, the carp headed straight toward the waterfall basin. In an instant the waters were swirling about, sucking it down like a leaf.

From the collection *Crackling Mountain*, translated from the Japanese by James O'Brien

A Scrap of Time

I want to talk about a certain time not measured in
months and years. For so long I have wanted to talk about
this time, and not in the way I will talk about it now, not just
about this one scrap of time. I wanted to, but I couldn't, I
didn't know how. I was afraid, too, that this second time,
which is measured in months and years, had buried the
other time under a layer of years, that this second time had
crushed the first and destroyed it within me. But no.
Today, digging around in the ruins of memory, I found it
fresh and untouched by forgetfulness. This time was
measured not in months but in a word – we no longer said
'in the beautiful month of May,' but 'after the first
"action," or the second, or right before the third.' We had
different measures of time, we different ones, always
different, always with that mark of difference that moved
some of us to pride and others to humility. We, who
because of our difference were condemned once again, as
we had been before in our history, we were condemned
once again during this time measured not in months nor by
the rising and setting of the sun, but by a word – 'action,' a
word signifying movement, a word you would use about a
novel or a play.

I don't know who used the word first, those who acted or
those who were the victims of their action; I don't know
who created this technical term, who substituted it for the
first term, 'round-up' – a word that became devalued (or
dignified?) as time passed, as new methods were

189

developed, and 'round-up' was distinguished from 'action' by the borderline of race. Round-ups were for forced labor.

We called the first action – that scrap of time that I want to talk about – a round-up, although no one was rounding anyone up; on that beautiful, clear morning, each of us made our way, not willingly, to be sure, but under orders, to the marketplace in our little town, a rectangle enclosed by high, crooked buildings – a pharmacy, clothing stores, an ironmonger's shop – and framed by a sidewalk made of big square slabs that time had fractured and broken. I have never again seen such huge slabs. In the middle of the marketplace stood the town hall, and it was right there, in front of the town hall, that we were ordered to form ranks.

I should not have written 'we,' for I was not standing in the ranks, although, obeying the order that had been posted the previous evening, I had left my house after eating a perfectly normal breakfast, at a table that was set in a normal way, in a room whose doors opened onto a garden veiled in morning mists, dry and golden in the rising sun.

Our transformation was not yet complete; we were still living out of habit in that old time that was measured in months and years, and on that lovely peaceful morning, filled with dry, golden mists, we took the words 'conscription of labor' literally, and as mature people tend to read between the lines, our imaginations replaced the word 'labor' with 'labor camp,' one of which, people said, was being built nearby. Apparently those who gave the order were perfectly aware of the poverty of our imaginations; that is why they saved themselves work by issuing a written order. This is how accurately they predicted our responses: after finishing a normal breakfast, at a normally set table, the older members of the family decided to disobey the order because they were afraid of the heavy physical labor, but they did not advise the young to do likewise – the young, who, if their disobedience were discovered, would not be able to plead old age. We were like infants.

This beautiful, clear morning that I am digging out of the ruins of my memory is still fresh; its colors and aromas have not faded: a grainy golden mist with red spheres of apples hanging in it, and the shadows above the river damp with the sharp odor of burdock, and the bright blue dress that I was wearing when I left the house and when I turned around at the gate. It was then, probably at that very moment, that I suddenly progressed, instinctively, from an infantile state to a still naive caution – instinctively, because I wasn't thinking about why I avoided the gate that led to the street and instead set off on a roundabout route, across the orchard, along the riverbank, down a road we called 'the back way' because it wound through the outskirts of town. Instinctively, because at that moment I still did not know that I wouldn't stand in the marketplace in front of the town hall. Perhaps I wanted to delay that moment, or perhaps I simply liked the river.

Along the way, I stopped and carefully picked out flat stones, and skipped them across the water; I sat down for a while on the little bridge, beyond which one could see the town, and dangled my legs, looking at my reflection in the water and at the willows that grew on the bank. I was not yet afraid then, nor was my sister. (I forgot to say that my younger sister was with me, and she, too, skipped stones across the water and dangled her legs over the river, which is called the Gniezna – a pitiful little stream, some eight meters wide.) My sister, too, was not yet afraid; it was only when we went further along the street, beyond the bridge, and the view of the marketplace leapt out at us from behind the building on the corner, that we suddenly stopped in our tracks.

There was the square, thick with people as on a market day, only different, because a market-day crowd is colorful and loud, with chickens clucking, geese honking, and people talking and bargaining. This crowd was silent. In a way it resembled a rally – but it was different from that, too. I don't know what it was exactly. I only know that we suddenly stopped and my sister began to tremble, and then

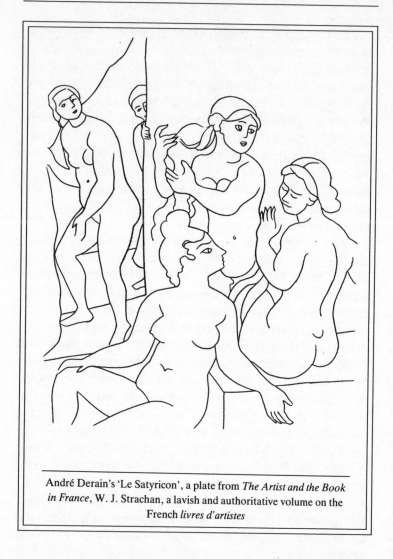

André Derain's 'Le Satyricon', a plate from *The Artist and the Book in France*, W. J. Strachan, a lavish and authoritative volume on the French *livres d'artistes*

I caught the trembling, and she said, 'Let's run away,' and although no one was chasing us and the morning was still clear and peaceful, we ran back to the little bridge, but we no longer noticed the willows or the reflections of our running figures in the water; we ran for a long time until we were high up the steep slope known as Castle Hill – the ruins of an old castle stood on top of it – and on this hillside, the jewel of our town, we sat down in the bushes, out of breath and still shaking.

From this spot we could see our house and our garden – it was just as it always was, nothing had changed – and we could see our neighbor's house, from which our neighbor had emerged, ready to beat her carpets. We could hear the slap slap of her carpet beater.

We sat there for an hour, maybe two, I don't know, because it was then that time measured in the ordinary way stopped. Then we climbed down the steep slope to the river and returned to our house, where we heard what had happened in the marketplace, and that our cousin David had been taken, and how they took him, and what message he had left for his mother. After they were taken away, he wrote down again what he had asked people to tell her; he threw a note out of the truck and a peasant brought it to her that evening – but that happened later. First we learned that the women had been told to go home, that only the men were ordered to remain standing there, and that the path chosen by our cousin had been the opposite of ours. We had been horrified by the sight of the crowd in the marketplace, while he was drawn towards it by an enormous force, a force as strong as his nerves were weak, so that somehow or other he did violence to his own fate, he himself, himself, himself, and that was what he asked people to tell his mother, and then he wrote it down: 'I myself am to blame, forgive me.'

We would never have guessed that he belonged to the race of the Impatient Ones, doomed to destruction by their anxiety and their inability to remain still, never – because he was round-faced and chubby, not at all energetic, the sort of person who can't be pulled away from his book, who smiles timidly, girlishly. Only the end of the war brought us the truth about his last hours. The peasant who delivered the note did not dare to tell us what he saw, and although other people, too, muttered something about what they had seen, no one dared to believe it, especially since the Germans offered proofs of another truth that each of us grasped at greedily; they measured out doses of it sparingly, with restraint – a perfect cover-up. They went to such trouble, created so many phantoms, that only time, time measured not in months and years, opened our eyes and convinced us.

Our cousin David had left the house later than we did, and when he reached the marketplace it was already known – not by everyone, to be sure, but by the so-called Council, which in time became the *Judenrat* – that the words 'conscription for labor' had nothing to do with a labor camp. One friend, a far-sighted older man, ordered the boy to hide just in case, and since it was too late to return home because the streets were blocked off, he led him to his own apartment in one of the houses facing the marketplace. Like us, not comprehending that the boy belonged to the race of the Impatient Ones, who find it difficult to cope with isolation and who act on impulse, he left David in a room that locked from inside. What our cousin experienced, locked up in that room, will remain forever a mystery. Much can be explained by the fact that the room had a view of the marketplace, of that silent crowd, of the faces of friends and relatives, and it may be that finally the isolation of his hiding place seemed to him more unbearable than the great and threatening unknown outside the window – an unknown shared by all who were gathered in the marketplace.

It was probably a thought that came in a flash: not to be alone, to be together with everyone. All that was needed was one movement of his hand.

I think it incorrect to assume that he left the hiding place because he was afraid that they would search the houses. That impatience of the heart, that trembling of the nerves, the burden of isolation, condemned him to extermination together with the first victims of our town.

He stood between a lawyer's apprentice and a student of architecture and to the question, 'Profession?' he replied,

'Teacher,' although he had been a teacher for only a short time and quite by chance. His neighbor on the right also told the truth, but the architecture student lied, declaring himself a carpenter, and this lie saved his life – or, to be more precise, postponed the sentence of death for two years.

Seventy people were loaded into trucks; at the last moment the rabbi was dragged out of his house – he was the seventy-first. On the way to the trucks they marched past the ranks of all those who had not yet managed to inform the interrogators about the work they did. It was then that our cousin said out loud, 'Tell my mother that it's my own fault and that I beg her forgiveness.' Presumably, he had already stopped believing what all of us still believed later: that they were going to a camp. He had that horrifying clarity of vision that comes just before death.

The peasant who that evening brought us the note that said, 'I myself am to blame, forgive me,' was somber and didn't look us in the eye. He said he had found the note on the road to Lubianki and that he didn't know anything else about it; we knew that he knew, but we did not want to admit it. He left, but he came back after the war to tell us what he had seen.

A postcard from the rabbi arrived two days later, convincing everyone that those who had been taken away were in a labor camp. A month later, when the lack of any further news began to make us doubt the camp, another postcard arrived, this one written by someone else who had been deported – an accountant, I think. After the postcard scheme came the payment of contributions: the authorities let it be understood that kilos of coffee or tea – or gold – would provide a family with news of their dear ones. As a gesture of compassion they also allowed people to send food parcels to the prisoners, who, it was said, were working in a camp in the Reich. Once again, after the second action, a postcard turned up. It was written in pencil and almost indecipherable. After this postcard, we said, 'They're done for.' But rumors told a different story altogether – of soggy earth in the woods by the village of Lubianki, and of a bloodstained handkerchief that had been found. These rumors came from nowhere; no eye-witnesses stepped forward.

The peasant who had not dared to speak at the time came back after the war and told us everything. It happened just as rumor had it, in a dense, overgrown forest, eight kilo-meters outside of town, one hour after the trucks left the marketplace. The execution itself did not take long; more time was spent on the preparatory digging of the grave.

At the first shots, our chubby, round-faced cousin David, who was always clumsy at gymnastics and sports, climbed a tree and wrapped his arms around the trunk like a child hugging his mother, and that was the way he died.

Title story from the collection *A Scrap of Time*, translated from the Polish by Madeline Levine and Francine Prose

Dust on Her Tongue

RODRIGO REY ROSA

Another one, she said to herself smiling. She was alone in what she took to be a sordid hotel room. The brick wall did not reach the ceiling, and a grey light came from the next room. She sat up in the sagging bed in which she was unable to sleep. The green pill which she put into her mouth had a bitter flavour, and she made a face as she swallowed it. She had no idea of where she was or of how she had got there. She was lost. But surely this was a hotel. A rooster crowed, and there was the diminishing sound of an automobile's engine in the distance. The bed seemed to move beneath her. Another pill.

In the morning she felt empty, without memory, and with an unpleasant sensation of having consumed too much alcohol. Her feet stuck out at the foot of the bed and her back ached. My god, my god, my god, she murmured, her voice low, ironic and desperate. The floor was of concrete but it was not cold. She pushed the door, which did not open entirely, and looked at the low grey sky. She was in the patio of a hotel she did not remember having entered. The doors to the rooms bore no numbers. She crossed the courtyard and went out into the street.

She remembered this street, paved with cobblestones. She had seen it the day before, but yesterday was very remote. It seemed to her she remembered the white walls, the tiled roofs. Had there been people in the street? It was a quiet town – too quiet. The silence was not natural, and she

197

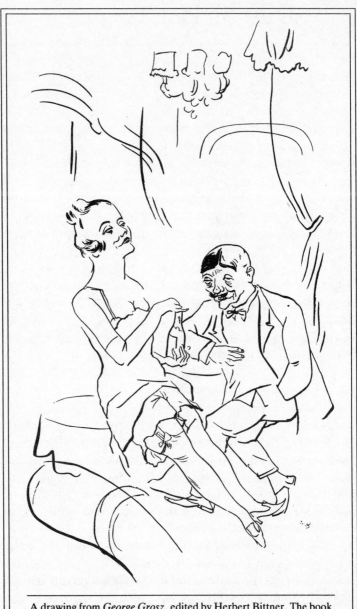

A drawing from *George Grosz*, edited by Herbert Bittner. The book
contained an essay 'On My Drawings' by the artist

knew it boded no good. She did not recall the name of the town.

Why did she see nobody? What day of the week was it? She counted on her fingers. Monday? Sunday? Monday, probably. For a town to be this silent on a Sunday would have upset her too much. The place was dead. She remembered that in the night a rooster had crowed, and that was some consolation, at least. Now she could hear the sound of her own footsteps on the stones. She came to the main square. At the end of the street she saw the side of a church. Something warned her not to go any nearer. She stood still and looked up and down the street. Then she turned and ran back leaving the plaza behind. A cry had come feebly from somewhere. The cry of a child? It had issued from inside the church, or had she imagined it? She ceased running, but continued to walk quickly, and stopped only when she had got inside the hotel. She shut the door, then reopened it to thrust her head out. The street was deserted.

She wanted to ask someone the name of this town. Where was the manager of the hotel?

Ave Maria, she said softly, not daring to call out. She had one hand on her bosom, and walked step by step across the vestibule, looking from side to side.

She remembered a bus filled with people. That was how she had come here. She stopped moving when she got to the gallery. Silence. This was a fourth-class establishment. Why had she spent the night here? She went across the patio to her room and sat down on the bed. She had no watch. Where was the sun? She looked at her hands. What had she done the night before?

A ditty, the words of a song. Yes. A room full of people, pine needles on the floor. A dance? Something she had wanted to forget. A man, the one who had given her the pills. It must be because of him that she was here. She studied the lines in her hand, as though something had been written there. She recalled a dirt road and a river that ran between mountains. It had been getting dark. She remembered that the little bus had jolted and made sudden turnings. But she could not remember getting into it, or what was supposed to be its destination. She did not know whether she had gone towards the north or the south. The memory of the road was rapidly growing dim; she did not want it to disappear, for fear of not finding it again.

She went out into the patio. With this dark sky the sun was invisible, and on the stone floor no object cast a shadow. It seemed as though all the rooms were empty. She heard footsteps from the direction of the street. Frightened, she ran into her room. As she shut the door it occurred to her that whatever was happening out there was something she preferred not to know about. Then she had a flash of recall which could have been the memory of a dream. With a stone in her hand, a heavy stone shaped like an egg, she had pounded the back of a man's head. She had given no warning. The man was her husband.

The sounds coming from the vestibule were men's voices, one of them high-pitched and shrill. They came across the gallery. There was knocking on the door of the adjoining room on the right. A moment later there came three sharp raps on her own door. She held her breath. The door opened.

Under the bed the air was foul. The sheet hung down from the edge of the bed to the floor, so that she could not see the feet of the person who had come in. She had left the bottle of pills on the bed, and she felt that the man had leaned over and picked it up. She heard him turn on his heels, and the door was shut. Now he knocked on the door of the room on the left.

She looked at the rolls of dust and the ancient spiderwebs which trembled with her breathing. She could not stay under there any longer. As the sound of the feet died away, she felt her fear becoming a sensation of discomfort and shame. Slowly she crawled out from under the bed. She wanted to find the reception clerk and pay her bill. She would go to the main square and get something to eat. Then she would find out when the next bus left for the city.

She tried to open the door, but it would not move. She pushed against it with her shoulder; she was locked in.

She did not want to kick the door or call out. She stood on the bed and looked over the top of the dividing wall: the space was too narrow for her body. She sat down. She was hungry and her mouth tasted like paper. She stared fixedly at the floor because she had remembered that before taking the bus she and her husband had been travelling in a plane. The size of the metal wing beneath her window had struck her as absurd. She felt that she had come so far on this trip that she would find it impossible to go back. She stood up and tried the door once more, pushing it with all her strength and kicking it. It was stronger than it looked. She shouted, and had the terrifying conviction that the shout remained in the room. She cried out again.

It was ridiculous! She was sure that it would be useless to complain to the proprietor. She hammered on the door with her fists. Someone had to come.

Overcome by fatigue, she suddenly stretched out on the bed. The wall was damp and smelled musty. Why was she so certain that she was in a hotel? The ceiling was too low. She shut her eyes, wishing that she had someone to massage her neck, which ached. She folded her hands over her abdomen and began to rub her stomach, in order to feel less hungry. She must be calm. It was not easy to lie still feeling nervous. She had clear memories, but they came from so long ago that she was unable to situate them in time. How old had she been the first time she saw her own face? She recalled the mirror's fancy frame.

Her mother had led her to the room which a few years later was to be hers. The curtains were drawn. Her dead grandmother seemed to be asleep in the bed. Her mother had carried her to the bed, and she had stretched out her hand and touched the nose, already cold. No, said her mother. Give her a kiss. She wondered whether dead people could hear. Now she ceased remembering, and listened for a sound. The light had grown weaker. The

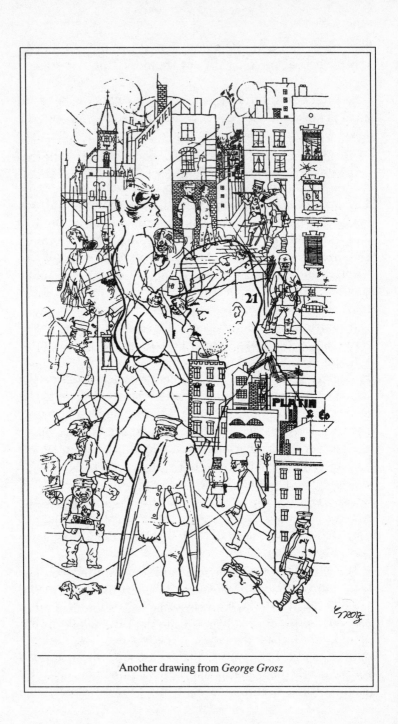

Another drawing from *George Grosz*

frozen face of her grandmother was telling her: You have died, too. You are dead.

Since she had become aware that the door was locked from the outside, since she had screamed and felt that her voice could not be heard, that idea had begun to work in her brain. Now it flashed through her and left her paralysed. She tried to raise her hand, was unable to, and this gave her a feeling of cold in her breast. The cold descended through her legs to her feet, and returned, as if it were something in her blood. Were her eyes open or shut? She blinked. Now there was no light.

How long had she been there? She could not believe it had been one day. The bed began to rock, and she sprang out of it. Beside herself, she rolled on the floor. She had heard a sound which had now become a roar. The floor also was rocking. She had hit her head. The legs of the bed squeaked.

I have to be dreaming, she told herself. I'm dead and I'm continuing to dream. The idea intrigued her. She imagined that somehow she would be able to follow, step by step, the process of her own decomposition. The flesh would turn into worms; the body would not feel, yet would be conscious. She would be composed of worms. It was the most humble form of transmigration imaginable, but at that moment it was enough. There was a sudden terrible racket. She jumped and fell backwards. She could not possibly be dead, she thought. Bits of earth fell from the ceiling. Were they burying her? I'm alive! she cried. And she repeated under her breath: I'm alive. There was dust on her tongue. She wanted to spit.

A few moments of calm. She did not want to open her eyes, but neither did she want to keep them shut. She began to feel sleepy, knowing that she should not fall asleep. It seemed to her that if she slept she would forget who she was, and that when she awoke she would have been changed into someone else: the tutelary goddess of a colony of worms. Madness. Finally she was overcome by sleep.

She came to. Two men were dragging her across the patio in a not too uncomfortable posture. She realized that she was not afraid of them. The warmth of their arms was reassuring: she was cold.

They went out into the street. The sky was red. She felt that she did not need the two men in order to walk, but she allowed them to go on supporting her. From time to time the earth trembled and there was that muffled roar that she had heard earlier. They went through a low door into a circular enclosure. The cloth walls moved in the wind. The men were young. One of them set to rubbing her arms and legs. Then he made her open her mouth so he could look inside.

Does your head ache?

Where am I? she said. What happened?

You may have a fractured skull, señora, although I don't think so. Try to be calm. I'll do what I can.

But I don't remember anything, she protested. Don't you understand?

Yes, I understand, he said. You'll remember.

From the centre of the ceiling hung a wire basket. There, among other objects which she recognized as hers, she saw the bottle of pills; it was the proof of an infraction she did not remember having committed. The owner of the hotel arrived to present her bill.

In the afternoon they told her that she would leave for the city, where her husband expected her. A rented car arrived to pick her up. They crossed the partially destroyed town. Men wearing green uniforms were beginning to clear away the rubble. The cornfields were ruined and the earth was the colour of ashes. Beside the road, on a treeless hill, a kneeling Indian was burning incense. He swung the burner and the smoke dissolved in the grey air.

Title story from the collection *Dust on Her Tongue*, translated from the Spanish by Paul Bowles

Alberta

CORA SANDEL

Grandmama is ill – dangerously ill. It says so in the telegram that is lying open and spread out on the living-room table.

Mama is going to travel to Grandmama. She ought to have gone long ago, when Grandmama was taken ill, but it's such an expensive journey.

When the telegram arrived Papa said that of course – of *course* – Mama must go, wherever the money was going to come from. Of course she must just do her packing and get ready.

But the worst of it is, Mama ought to have gone long ago, and now she may get there too late, even though the boat is leaving in a couple of hours.

She goes up to pack, sniffling. Her eyes are red and her lips pressed tightly together. Every now and then she expels a long, deep sigh.

Papa has disappeared into his study. The atmosphere is stormy.

Alberta dithers around the suitcase, attempting to make herself useful and, if possible, to dissipate the storm. She doesn't know what to do with her cold hands, and wrings them as if freezing. With all her strength she exerts herself to appear sympathetic towards Mama, but her conscience is guilty, because all the time she is thinking about Papa in his study.

'Isn't there anything I can help you with?' She tries cautiously, since the last thing that happened was that Mama irritably took something which Alberta had brought her straight out of her hands and put it back on the table.

'No, thank you, my dear Alberta,' she said in that cold, bitter voice which Alberta dreads more than anything. 'You're only getting in my way. Leave me alone.'

Now Alberta knows very well that it will be wrong if she does leave her alone. Her palms are beginning to sweat. She moves out of Mama's way and keeps as quiet as possible.

Suddenly Mama, kneeling in front of the suitcase with her face bent over it, exclaims, 'And your father doesn't think of giving me a single little thing for the journey, Alberta. Never the least thoughtfulness – never the slightest little attention. I can't tell you how much it hurts me, now when I need to feel a little love about me. I feel so lonely, so lonely.'

Mama's voice is choked with sobs, and Alberta watches the tears roll slowly down over her cheekbones and disappear into the suitcase.

Then Mama puts in Grandmama's photograph.

'Like this picture of your grandmother, Alberta. It's been standing on the bedside table for years, getting faded and ugly and ruined, but it has never occurred to your father to give me a little frame for it. Only a small thing, of course, but. . . .'

Mama sniffs into the suitcase.

Alberta wrings her hands so that they risk being put out of joint. If her life were to depend on it, she would not know what to answer. When Mama calls Papa 'your father', it's like a warning bell.

Suddenly a door opens and someone calls 'Alberta!'

It's Papa.

When Alberta enters the study he is standing at his desk, holding a five-kroner piece in one hand. In the other is his open wallet. Alberta approaches him, her heart thumping.

'Look, Alberta,' says Papa, 'here's five kroner. Could

you find some little thing for Mama that she might like to have on the journey? A small bottle of eau-de-Cologne, perhaps? I thought she might like it, and then I thought that now you're such a big girl, Alberta, you might go and buy it for Papa. I have so much to do, you know.'

Alberta catches her breath for relief and joy. *Could* she go and buy that little thing? Of course she could.

'Yes,' she says eagerly, 'of course I can. But I know of something that Mama wants much more than eau-de-Cologne, Papa.'

'What's that, Alberta?'

'She'd like a frame for Grandmama's picture,' exclaims Alberta, terrified lest she may not get it.

'Yes,' says Papa, 'but I'm sure she'd prefer some eau-de-Cologne for the journey. She can always have a frame some other time.'

'Oh no, Papa, no! I know she wants a frame. Nothing would please her more than a frame.'

'All right, all right,' says Papa. 'If you think so. Do as you think. That's the best thing, Alberta. I have so much work to do, as you see.'

Papa gestures at the desk and sits down. And he rubs his glasses before positioning them in front of his reddened eyes, which always look so tired.

Alberta reassures him yet again, 'Yes, Papa, yes', and hurries out.

After a while she returns from the hardware store on the corner with a piece of thick, polished glass which, with the help of a prop behind it, stands on two brass knobs. She has chosen it instead of all kinds of frames with metal scrolls and flourishes, and she feels certain she has chosen with good taste. She creeps on tiptoe through the kitchen and hall into Papa's study.

'Yes,' says Papa, looking at the object over his glasses, 'it's all right, but . . . I must say I think it would have been better to get some eau-de-Cologne,' he adds. 'But take it in to Mama, then. You go in and give it her, Alberta. You can say it's from you children.'

Alberta goes out quietly and hangs up her coat. Then she goes in to Mama through the dining-room.

Mama looks up from the suitcase. The barometer is quite unmistakably pointing to storm.

'Ah, there you are. May I ask where you've been? Not one of you thinks of giving me any help, not even you, Alberta. I thought I could count on a little help from my big daughter, but I see I was mistaken. You all leave me alone to. . . .'

Mama's voice is lost in a sob.

'Mama,' says Alberta, feeling a choking sensation in her throat that makes it difficult to get the words out. 'Mama, I've been to buy this for you.'

'What is it?' says Mama, and her voice is so cold. Oh, Mama's cold voice. She takes the packet and unwraps the paper.

'Whatever is this? But, my dear Alberta . . . ?'

'It's, it's,' stammers Alberta, her composure already lost. 'It was Papa who – but then I said that I thought. . . . It's from us children. . . .'

She gets no further, for Mama interrupts her. 'What an extraordinary idea! If only he had bought a little eau-de-Cologne or something nice for the journey – the kind of thing other husbands think of when their wives travel.'

Mama's voice is like ice.

But inside Alberta something is jumping so oddly. Now she can feel that strange, painful pressure in her chest, as if her heart were turning over. And then will come the tears, that violent weeping that she cannot control. She knows it will. It's in her throat already, as she turns and runs out through the door.

Nothing irritates Mama more than Alberta's weeping.

And she rushes out and grabs the key to the only place where she can whimper and sob her heart out without embarrassing anyone.

From the collection *The Silken Thread*, translated from the Norwegian by Elizabeth Rokkan

A drawing from *Hebdomeros*, Giorgio de Chirico. The only novel by the famous artist

Hebdomeros

GIORGIO DE CHIRICO

And then began the tour of that strange building situated in a street that looked forbidding, although it was distinguished and not gloomy. As seen from the street the building was reminiscent of a German consulate in Melbourne. Its ground floor was entirely taken up with large stores. Although it was neither Sunday nor a holiday, the stores were closed, endowing this part of the street with an air of tedium and melancholy, a certain desolation, that particular atmosphere which pervades Anglo-Saxon towns on Sundays. A slight smell of docks hung in the air; the indefinable and highly suggestive smell that emanates from dockside warehouses in ports. The German-consulate-at-Melbourne look was a purely personal association on the part of Hebdomeros and when he mentioned it to his friends they smiled and found the comparison amusing, but they didn't dwell on the point, and immediately spoke of something else, which led Hebdomeros to decide that they had probably not grasped the meaning of what he had said. And he reflected on the difficulty of making yourself understood once you begin to develop at a certain height or depth. It's odd, Hebdomeros repeated to himself, the idea that something had escaped me would keep me awake, but most people can see, hear or read things which are totally obscure to them without feeling upset.

They began to climb the staircase which was very broad and built entirely of polished wood; in the centre was a carpet; at the foot of the staircase was a little Doric column carved in oak, which incorporated the end of the stair rail, and on it stood a polychrome statue, also made of wood, representing a Californian negro with his arms raised above his head, holding a gas lamp, its jet covered with an asbestos handle. Hebdomeros felt he was going up to see a dentist or a specialist in venereal diseases; and he felt he was developing stomach-ache; he tried to overcome these feelings by remembering that he was not alone, that two friends were with him, strong, athletic young men, carrying automatics with spare ammunition in the gun-pockets of their trousers. When they realized that they were approaching the floor that was said to produce the greatest number of strange apparitions they began to go up more slowly and on tiptoe; their gaze became more attentive. They moved slightly farther apart, while remaining on the same level, so that they could go down the stairs again freely and as quickly as possible, if some apparition of a special kind forced them to do so.

At this moment Hebdomeros thought of his childhood dreams, when he would go anxiously up wide and dimly lit staircases of polished wood where the carpet in the centre muffled the sound of his footsteps (his shoes, moreover, even outside dreams, rarely squeaked because he had his shoes made to measure by a shoemaker called Perpignani who was known all over the town for his good quality leather; Hebdomeros's father, however, had no talent for buying himself shoes; the ones he wore made horrible noises as though he were crushing sackfuls of hazelnuts at every step).

Then the bear appeared, the disturbing, obstinate bear who followed you up and down the stairs and across corridors, with his head down and apparently thinking of other things; the desperate flight across bedrooms with complicated exits, the leap through the window into the void (suicide while dreaming) and the descent in hovering flight, reminiscent of those condormen whom Leonardo enjoyed drawing among the catapults and anatomical frag-

ments. It was a dream which always predicted unpleasant-
ness and above all illness.

'Here we are!' said Hebdomeros, stretching out his arms
in front of his companions in the classic gesture made by
temporizing captains arresting the onward rush of their
soldiers. They reached the threshold of a vast room with a
high ceiling, decorated in the style of 1880; the lighting and
general atmosphere of the room, which was totally devoid
of furniture, were reminiscent of the gaming rooms at
Monte Carlo. In a corner, two gladiators wearing diving
helmets were exercising without conviction under the
bored gaze of a master, a pensioned ex-gladiator with a
vulturelike eye and a scarred body.

'*Gladiators*! This word contains an enigma,' said
Hebdomeros in a low voice to the younger of his two
companions. And he thought of the music halls with
illuminated ceilings evoking visions of Dante's paradise; he
thought also of those afternoons in Rome, as the show
came to an end and the huge velarium increased the shade
over the arena with its smell of sawdust and blood-soaked
sand.

> Vision of Rome, coolness of antiquity
> Anxiety of twilight, song of the sea.

More padded doors and short, deserted corridors, and
then all at once: *Society! Go into the fashionable world.*
Lead *a fashionable life.* The *rules* of society. *Savoir vivre.*
Invitation TTYL (to take your leave). DP (deliver personally). PTO (please turn over).

In a corner of the drawing-room was a huge grand piano,
open; without standing on tiptoe you could see its complicated entrails and the clear anatomy of its interior. But it
was easy to imagine what a catastrophe it would have been
if one of those chandeliers laden with pink and blue wax
candles had fallen into the piano with all its candles alight.
What a tragedy within the melogenic gulf! Wax running
along the metallic wires, as taut as the bow of Ulysses,

hindering the precise action of the little felt-covered hammers.

'It's better not to think of it,' said Hebdomeros, turning towards his companions, and then all three of them, holding each other's hands, as though confronting some danger, gazed with silent concentration at this surprising spectacle; they saw themselves as passengers in a perfected submarine, surprising, as they looked through the portholes, the mysteries of the oceanic fauna and flora. Moreover, the spectacle which met their eyes really possessed an underwater quality. It was reminiscent of large aquaria, if only because of the diffused lighting which removed shadows. A strange and inexplicable silence hung over the entire scene: the pianist, seated at his instrument, playing *without making a sound*; the pianist whom after all one did not see for there was nothing about him fit to be seen, and those dramatic figures moving round the piano, with cups of coffee in their hands, making gestures and movements as in slow-motion films of athletes jumping. All those people lived in a world of their own, a world apart: they were unaware of everything; they had never heard of the war in the Transvaal nor of the Martinique catastrophe; they did not recognize you because they had never met you before; they did not worry about anything and nothing had any power over them: neither prussic acid, nor the stiletto, nor armoured bullets. If a *rebel* (let us call him this) had thought of lighting the fuse of an infernal machine, the hundred pounds of melinite contained in the device would have burnt away slowly, hissing like damp logs. It was enough to make you despair. Hebdomeros maintained that it was the effect of the *milieu* and the atmosphere and that he knew no way of changing it all; the only thing to do was to live and let live. But, *that is the question*, were they really alive? It would have been very difficult to give an answer, especially like this, at once, without spending several nights of deep meditation on the subject, as Hebdomeros did whenever a complex problem preoccupied his mind.

And then he was also afraid of starting a discussion with

his friends on the eternal questions: What is life? What is death? Is life possible on another planet? Do you believe in metempsychosis, the immortality of the soul, the inviolability of natural laws, in ghosts who forecast the onset of calamities, in the existence of the subconscious in dogs, in the dreams of owls, in all that is enigmatic in crickets, quails' heads and the spots on a leopard's skin? He detested this kind of discussion, although at bottom he felt himself instinctively attracted by the enigmatic side of beings and things. But it was the others who inspired mistrust in him; he feared their *amour propre*, their resentment, their hysteria; he did not want to arouse complex feelings in his friends. Besides, he also feared their admiration; all these cries of *It's fantastic! It's unheard of! It's amazing!* caused him no more than a very indifferent pleasure and in the end irritated him. His only happiness occurred when nobody paid any attention to him; to be dressed like everyone else, to pass unnoticed, never to feel on his back or in his side the arrow of a gaze, even benevolent. Or else, yes, he would have liked people to take notice of him, but in a *totally different way*. To have the advantages and satisfaction of fame without its drawbacks. To be a Sybarite, in fact!

From *Hebdomeros*, translated from the French by Margaret Crosland

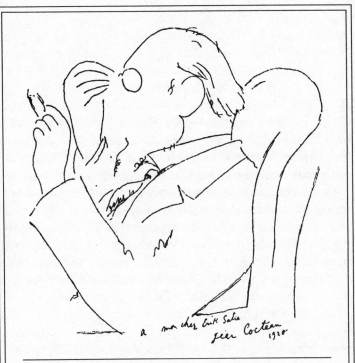

Jean Cocteau's drawing of the composer Erik Satie from *Cocteau's World: an Anthology of His Writings* (edited by Margaret Crosland, various translators)

Three Score Years and Ten

PETER VANSITTART

I am nearing my seventieth birthday and people have begun, so to speak, tapping me like a barometer or offering an arm to help me across a yard of floor. Solemnity protrudes from those anxious to pack me away; I demur, yet only genius disregards such a date and, lacking this, I brood over a wry story told by Angus Wilson. He was at work in his garden and a child peered in. 'Look, Mummy, there's an old man writing!' 'Yes, darling, it does them so much good.' At dinner, recently, a stranger addressed me: 'I associate you with the fifties. You must find it rather nice to feel your work is really finished, you can sit back and never write another line.' This was not the sort of remark to appeal to one still busy producing for an exceptional publishing house with a more cheerful date to celebrate.

For years, I usually fancied myself the youngest present; now, if not actually on crutches, I assume that I am the oldest and, in some distorted instinct for survival, tend to exaggerate my age rather boastfully, so that 'when I was young' hints at ages biblical or Minoan. 'Yes, I remember the *Titanic*, and as she sailed past I couldn't help thinking. . . .' I do remember the General Strike: grey queues, distant shouts, young men with curious, vaguely sinister, claims ('I collared a tram'), the familiar turning strange, the postman in unusual costume ignoring my greeting. At Haig's death, breakfast faces were frozen solid but from the kitchen sounded chuckles. One memory is of being taken to see Father Christmas at a department store, but,

Full-page drawing from *Hidden Faces*, Salvador Dali's only novel.
The drawing is inspired by Gala, the painter's wife

alas for innocence, seeing two Father Christmases, beery, smelly, quarrelling obscenely about demarcation rights, a bizarre conflict that forever safeguarded me against disappointments, making me wary of reputation, fashion, status. Later, 'Spanish Republic' seemed to me a contradiction, Sartre over-rated, Brecht's proletarian jacket too well tailored. I agreed with Walter Scott who, according to John Buchan, when told that something 'was in accordance with the spirit of the age', replied that the spirit of the age might be a lying spirit. Ramsay MacDonald's impressive diction, his grave warning against clipping the wings of the rising tide, made politics appear a constant fight to the last ditch with one's back to the wall. In contrast was the great humanitarian, Nansen, whom Gorky called the conscience of Europe. When told a rescue job was impossible he went out and did it, showing throughout that agnosticism is no bar to sainthood.

My young intelligence was tested by pre-war sages announcing, though from India and California, that Hitler was best overcome by meditation and deep breathing. Ezra Pound, whose brilliance of sound, colour, line, 'news that stays news' was stimulating me, was yet sneering at 'Mr Jewsevelt'; Mosley bellowed that fascism alone guaranteed free speech in Britain. More pleasantly, I saw Hobbs and Woolley bat, and the music hall of Billy Bennett, 'Almost a Gentleman', Ernie Lottingar, admired by T. S. Eliot, and Norman Long: 'Lady Astor's bonnet / Had a Guinness advert on it / On the day that Chelsea went and won the Cup.'

My social sympathies have culpably slackened, I am not howling against poll tax and Mike Gatting or making myself spokesman for those who have never heard of me, though the crowds on the Berlin Wall and Mandela upright amongst the seething, potentially dangerous crowds made me tearful. Village politics is another matter but I have long lost the impetuosity with which I once wrote for Orwell in *Tribune*, imagining myself Gracchus or Wat Tyler. European revolutionaries since 1789, fixated on the

Marat/Robespierre twaddle about the 'Despotism of Liberty' have, I am now convinced, done more harm than good, periodically reducing the population. 'Only I am right' also means 'To the guillotine'. Here at home, they have not disproved Chesterton's observation that the English are more interested in the inequality of horses than the equality of man.

This tiresome birthday, however, induces mild personal stocktaking, rather than political or mystical speculation. I respect the Swedish theologian, the Revd Krister Stendahl. 'I happen to believe that the whole long and glorious Christian tradition of speaking about the immortality of the soul is only a period of the Judeo-Christian tradition, and that period may soon be ending. The word immortality occurs in two places in the New Testament; once about God, "who alone has immortality", and once in a very special setting, where it is perhaps borrowed from other people whom Paul quotes when he speaks of how the mortal nature must put on immortality. My point is that the whole world which comes to us through the Bible is not interested in the immortality of the soul.'

Defensively, I remind myself that years are inventions of priests, daughters of Zeus. AD 2000 will produce high-flown or hysterical verbiage about entropy, yet the date has no strict significance. Real birthdays are memorable occasions, vital initiations, rebirth-days. I have had, say, fourteen. First day at school, certain deaths and encounters, losing virginity, newsreels of monstrous camps, my first book, my first serious review – by Francis King, who, discussing me in the *Listener* alongside Mauriac and Prokosch, gave me a necessary grain of confidence. Flaubert (I think) put it differently, that with cheek a man can get on in the world. Thenceforward, though I often stood at the ironic mirror, murmuring 'others are better', I have somehow survived on the literary fringes, despite lack of careerist acumen, which will not now develop. When Chatto accepted my first novel, in 1941, they invited me to meet their Literary Adviser (a title now obsolete), V. S.

Pritchett. He had noted certain faults, proposed certain alterations. I was outraged. Faults? There were none. Alterations? Nonsense. Fundamentally, I was overawed. Pritchett's *New Statesman* essays, 'Books in General', were for me a one-man university revealing immeasurable vistas, yet making me imagine a vast authoritarian figure set to demolish my masterpiece and too closely resembling the Wodehouse headmaster reputed to chew broken bottles and devour his young. Those who know and revere V.S.P., that stocky benign presence, that twinkling curiosity, will gape at this, but, crassly, I allowed some years to pass before meeting him – another birthday – and renewing my apprenticeship. 'The traditional gift of the Russian novelist is for recording the off-moments and lost hours of the day.' I should have learnt this earlier.

My next novel won praise from Pamela Hansford Johnson, and Orwell's genial successor, T. R. Fyvel, considered that to meet her would do me no harm at all. Actually, it did. I sent her a nervous card, she invited me for a drink. Cocoa. Never mind. She was flattering, informative, kind. Then she remarked that the coming novelist was one C. P. Snow. Chary of confessing total ignorance of this paragon I insisted that he wrote irredeemable trash. She cooled with the cocoa, and next week I read with some interest of their engagement. Not long after, I met a fat man and, still a pompous youth, told him that he spoke very well on a number of interesting subjects and should try his hand at authorship. The fat man, J. B. Priestley, was markedly unamused.

Life has proved, so to speak, excitingly commonplace. Periodic descents to the underworld, with returns not dazzling but stolid. I am dogged by unkindness to one girl, timidity with another; by a letter from my divorced wife announcing her terminal cancer. 'But I can't expect you to be interested.' In much pain, I realize, is much retribution. Yet I have marvellous friends, generous ex-pupils, a stable and finalizing love. Some of my books have been published, the best of them by Peter Owen, and are to be found in hospitable households, the bookmarkers firmly attached to page four. Their comparative failure early inoculated me against grand delusions, and against chatterboxes who tell me in bad prose how to write, earning money for doing little, like Regency parsons. Freed from grosser ambitions, I am left free to write only what I wish to. Independence is not only worth an empire, it *is* an empire.

I may yet reach Babylon, if only by candlelight. Flesh withers, imagination remains, freedom indeed enlarges. 'You cannot', a boy lectures me, 'afford not to read Ian McEwan.' But I can. I will never have to read Smollett, study neo-deconstructionalism, pretend to understand Heidegger. Instead, I can re-read Mann, Proust, Faulkner, T. H. White, perhaps for the last time. Envy has departed. There are books I would like to have written, but chiefly am glad that they exist: *Testament*, *A Legacy*, *Late Call*, *Instead of a Letter*, *Mani*, *The Virgin in the Garden*, *The Aunt's Story*, *The Man Who Invented Tomorrow*, *No Country for Young Men*, *A Question of Loyalties*. The authors, of course, I need not name. The Novel remains for me the finest of instruments; I would rather have written *The Brothers Karamazov* than *The Waste Land*.

The past has not yet shrivelled, nor need the future. My most recent book has improved on its predecessor and, though set in AD 275, sums up my conclusions of a longish life, at least showing that impulses can still stir. Back in 1935 I read a sentence by H. G. Wells: 'A chill had come over the pride and confidence of Rome. In AD 270–275, Rome, which had been an open and secure city for three centuries, was fortified by the Emperor Aurelian.' Just this, but it haunted me until last year when, pushing up like a mushroom through concrete, it became a novel, *The Wall*, which Peter Owen published last summer.

Work never finishes: if it does, one refuses to admit it and works the harder, without toadying either to past or future. The present still glitters with brilliant detail. Oddities appear whenever needed. In Surrey lives a gentleman who disproves the fingerprint method; in Norfolk another, not, as might be expected, short, olive-skinned, testy, but fair, lanky, complacent, who boasts that he has at last put Corsica on the map. To sharpen my narrative skill, hitherto weak, I am attempting a thriller, not for publication. It may take two 'years'.

In Suffolk, a friend has recently given me a bicycle: adventure, discoveries and, after the punctures, long, healthy trudges. Also, more dangerous, a TV set: nostalgia, endless wallowing in the stately *non sequiturs* of Laurel and Hardy and the nuances of Bette Davis's first film. Both will give Fate a nudge. At whatever age, the art of life is in transforming set-backs to assets, transforming moribund selves. To date, happiness? On the whole, yes. Contentment? On the whole, no. I may reach fifteen – fifteen major events in life: not outstanding, not too bad.

c'est la vie!

Drawing from *Some Are More Human Than Others*, Stevie Smith. A sketchbook of witty illustrations to overheard phrases and scraps of conversation

"This beautiful
face touches across
the centuries, it is
so subtle and
yielding, yet
innocent. Her name
is Lucrezia Borgia."

"Yes, I know. I
knew her brother
once — but only for a short time."

Another drawing from *Some Are More Human Than Others*, Stevie
Smith

Independent / for Peter Owen

A sea-fog muffed the offshore bell-buoy's cone.
At sixteen, truant, reading on the beach,
I'd found your books and fished for the logo,
ransacked our library shelves to be alone

with what I'd found: Pavese, Cocteau, Gide —
a concentration on an imagery
that brought poetry into the novel,
a universal dynamic that freed

me of the dead post-fifties legacy,
the English rot, novels stacked to be pulped.
You had De Sade, Mishima, Hermann Hesse,
a reckless, dare-all sensibility

that's stood out four decades, a singular
devotion to what's good and lives as that;
no compromise, just the resolution
to find in a nebula the one star

that's compact, resonant; a line vibrates
if it's in tune. You had a typewriter
and five hundred pounds as a beginning,
and a sympathy which communicates

to the committed, for they find in you
the mirror of themselves; integrity,
defiance of corporate publishing.
The mist recedes, and now the bay is blue

again in memory. You fed my youth
with inspired risks which are continuous;
and now your name is everywhere with those
who value imagination as truth.

Jeremy Reed

225

COME, DEATH

I feel ill. What can the matter be?
I'd ask God to have pity on me,
But I turn to the one I know, and say:
Come, Death, and carry me away.

Ah me, sweet Death, you are the only god
Who comes as a servant when he is called, you know,
Listen then to this sound I make, it is sharp,
Come Death. Do not be slow.

96

The final page of *Some Are More Human Than Others*, Stevie Smith.
This is her last poem

Notes on the
Authors and Illustrators

Jane Bowles was born in New York in 1917 and died in Malaga in 1973. She was married to the writer Paul Bowles, with whom she lived in various parts of the world. At the age of twenty-one she wrote the novel *Two Serious Ladies*; she is also the author of a volume of stories entitled *Plain Pleasures* and a play, *In the Summer House*, all available in *The Collected Works of Jane Bowles* (Peter Owen). Her international reputation has escalated since her death.

Paul Bowles was born in New York in 1910 and came to Europe in 1931 to study music with Aaron Copland. In 1938 he married **Jane Bowles** (née Auer). After the war they settled in Tangier, which is still Paul Bowles's permanent home. His novel *The Sheltering Sky* has become a contemporary classic and has been filmed by Bernardo Bertolucci. Bowles is the author of several novels, collections of short stories and volumes of autobiography.

Marc Chagall (1887–1985), one of the greatest twentieth-century painters, was born in Vitebsk in western Russia and spent much of his later life in Paris and southern France, as well as in the United States. His early autobiography, *My Life*, first appeared in 1947.

Giorgio de Chirico was born in Greece in 1888 of Italian parents. *Hebdomeros*, first published in France in 1929, is the painter's only novel. The drawings that illustrate it are from around the same period. A profound influence on the Surrealist movement, he died in 1977.

Jean Cocteau (1889–1963), the great French man of letters, was active in ballet, music and films as well as literature. *The Impostor* and *Les Enfants terribles* are regarded as among the best of his novels. He was also a gifted artist.

Sidonie Gabrielle Colette, the author of over fifty books, was born in Saint-Sauveur-en-Puisaye in Burgundy in 1873 and died in Paris in 1954. The publication of *Chéri* and *La fin de Chéri* established her as a major talent.

Salvador Dali was born in Spain in 1904 and died there in 1989. A major Surrealist painter, he wrote only one novel, *Hidden Faces*.

Osamu Dazai was born in 1909 into a wealthy family in northern Japan. His best-known novels are *The Setting Sun* and *No Longer Human*, which were both published in Britain by Peter Owen, as was *Crackling Mountain*, a selection of his short stories. Notorious for his dissolute, bohemian lifestyle, Dazai committed suicide in 1948

Shusaku Endo was born in Tokyo in 1923. After the war he studied in France until obliged to return to Japan due to ill-health. He has written many books and his novel *Silence* is acclaimed as a masterpiece. Endo is a Roman Catholic and Christianity features in his writing. He is regarded as Japan's leading contemporary novelist.

Erté (1892–1990) was born Romain de Tirtoff in St Petersburg. He moved to Paris in 1912 and became one of the most sought-after designers in theatre, opera and film. He is particularly noted for his extravagant costumes and tableaux for the Folies-Bergère. Peter Owen published his autobiography, *Things I Remember*.

Ida Fink was born in Poland in 1921. Her music studies were interrupted by the Nazi Occupation, and she lived in a ghetto before going into hiding until the end of the war. She now lives in Israel with her family. *A Scrap of Time* was her first book. The title story appeared in *The New Yorker* and the collection itself was awarded the first Anne Frank Prize for Literature.

Hermann Hesse was born in Germany in 1877 and died in 1962. A recipient of the Nobel Prize for Literature, he wrote poetry, short stories and criticism as well as novels. He achieved considerable success among the post-war generation with works such as *Demian* and *Siddhartha*.

Anna Kavan was born about 1901 and died in London in 1968. She was a heroin addict for most of her life and her addiction and bouts of mental illness feature prominently in her writing. *Ice* (1967) is widely regarded as her most significant work. The author of a number of novels and oustanding short stories, some of which were published after her death, Anna Kavan is now receiving belated critical recognition.

Paul Klee was born in Berne in 1879 and died near Locarno in 1940. His paintings and etchings are notable for their intensely personal blend of fantasy and wit and he amassed a remarkable *œuvre* of more than 9,000 works. Peter Owen published *The Diaries of Paul Klee* in 1965.

Anaïs Nin was born in Paris in 1903 of Cuban, French and Danish descent, and lived in the USA and Europe. Her first book was a collection of stories, *Under a Glass Bell*, and this was followed by other fiction. Nin is perhaps best known for her *Journals*, which were published by Peter Owen and which finally established her reputation. She died in the United States in 1977.

Cesare Pavese, one of Italy's most famous writers, was born near Cuneo in Piedmont in 1908. He published novels, short stories and poetry and was also distinguished as a translator of English and American authors, including Dickens. He committed suicide in 1950.

Octavio Paz, who was born in Mexico in 1914, is one of the finest contemporary poets writing in Spanish. He is also a philosopher, essayist and critic, and was formerly his country's ambassador to India. In 1990 he was awarded the Nobel Prize for Literature.

James Purdy was born in Ohio. His first novel, *63: Dream Palace*, was published in Britain in 1957 to great critical acclaim. Since then he has written poetry, plays and short stories as well as novels. He now lives in Brooklyn and teaches at New York University.

Jeremy Reed was born in Jersey. He has published poetry, fiction and a critical work, *Madness – The Price of Poetry* (Peter Owen). His poetry collection *By the Fisheries* earned him the Somerset Maugham Award in 1985.

Rodrigo Rey Rosa was born in Guatemala in 1958 and commutes between that country, New York and Tangier. His first book, *The Beggar's Knife*, was followed by *Dust on Her Tongue*; both were translated by **Paul Bowles**.

Cora Sandel was born in Oslo in 1880 and spent part of her life in France and Italy. She died in Sweden in 1974. Best known for the novels in her *Alberta* trilogy, she is often compared to **Colette**, whose books she translated into Norwegian and whose feminist sympathies she shared.

Stevie Smith (1902–1971) was born in Hull and brought up in Palmers Green, north London, where she lived for most of her life. She is best remembered as a poet but was also the author of three novels, including *Novel on Yellow Paper*.

Roland Topor was born in Paris in 1938 of Polish/Jewish descent. He has made several films and his paintings and drawings have been widely exhibited. Peter Owen published his book *Stories and Drawings* in 1968.

Peter Vansittart, who was born in 1920, is the author of more than twenty novels, ten of which have been published by Peter Owen. He has also written non-fiction and children's books. His autobiographical book, *Paths from a White Horse*, was published in 1985 and received high praise from critics.

Tarjei Vesaas (1897–1976) was one of Norway's foremost twentieth-century writers. He spent much of his life in semi-seclusion in the Norwegian countryside where he was born. Repeatedly a Nobel Prize candidate, he wrote many books, including *The Birds*, *A Boat in the Evening* and *The Ice Palace*, which won the Nordic Council Prize.

Authors
We Have Published

James Agee
Bella Akhmadulina
Tariq Ali
Kenneth Allsop
Alfred Andersch
Guillaume Apollinaire
Machado de Assis
Miguel Angel Asturias

Duke of Bedford
Thomas Blackburn
Jane Bowles
Paul Bowles
Ilse, Countess von Bredow
Lenny Bruce

Finn Carling
Blaise Cendrars
Marc Chagall
Giorgio de Chirico
Uno Chiyo
Jean Cocteau
Colette
Richard Corson
Benedetto Croce
Margaret Crosland
e. e. cummings

Salvador Dali
Osamu Dazai
Anita Desai
Autran Dourado
Lawrence Durrell

Sergei Eisenstein
Shusaku Endo
Erté

Knut Faldbakken
Ida Fink
Wolfgang Georg Fischer

Carlo Emilio Gadda
Michel Gauquelin
André Gide
Natalia Ginzburg
Jean Giono
Geoffrey Gorer
William Goyen
Julien Gracq
Robert Graves
Julien Green
George Grosz

Barbara Hardy
H.D.
Rayner Heppenstall
David Herbert
Gustaw Herling
Hermann Hesse
King Hussein of Jordan

Yasushi Inoue

Hans Henny Jahnn
Karl Jaspers

Takeshi Kaiko
Anna Kavan
Yasunari Kawabata
Nikos Kazantzakis
Christer Kihlman
Paul Klee

James Laughlin
Violette Leduc

József Lengyel
Robert Liddell
Francisco García Lorca

André Maurois
Henri Michaux
Henry Miller
Marga Minco
Yukio Mishima
Margaret Morris
Angus Wolfe Murray

Gérard de Nerval
Anaïs Nin

Yoko Ono
Uri Orlev

Marco Pallis
Boris Pasternak
Cesare Pavese
Octavio Paz
Mervyn Peake
Carlo Pedretti
Dame Margery Perham
Edith Piaf
Fiona Pitt-Kethley
Ezra Pound
Marcel Proust
James Purdy

Graciliano Ramos
Jeremy Reed
Rodrigo Rey Rosa
Joseph Roth

Marquis de Sade
Cora Sandel

George Santayana
May Sarton
Jean-Paul Sartre
Ferdinand de Saussure
Gerald Scarfe
Albert Schweitzer
George Bernard Shaw
Isaac Bashevis Singer
Edith Sitwell
Stevie Smith
C. P. Snow
Vladimir Soloukhin
Natsume Soseki
Muriel Spark
Prunella Stack
Gertrude Stein
Bram Stoker

Rabindranath Tagore
Tambimuttu
Elisabeth Russell Taylor
Anne Tibble
Roland Topor

Anne Valery
Peter Vansittart
José J. Veiga
Tarjei Vesaas
Noel Virtue

Max Weber
William Carlos Williams
Phyllis Willmott
Monique Wittig

A. B. Yehoshua
Marguerite Young